THERE IS NO "MAGIC" IN GOOD WRITING

For all too many, good writing seems a gift reserved for the "talented" few. Yet this is far from the case. Writing is a skill that can be mastered by anyone willing to learn its relatively few basic principles, and to put them into action.

With superb clarity, this book strips away the mystery from writing. It illumines the uses—and misuses—of words, sentences, paragraphs, and themes, and provides expertly designed exercises to insure thorough understanding. As an added bonus, in showing both student and layman how to write more easily and effectively, it offers telling insight into the art of clear thinking, which is the necessary complement of —THE LIVELY ART OF WRITING

LUCILE VAUGHAN PAYNE brings to this volume the authoritative voice of a professional writer, and the knowledge of an experienced teacher. She has been a successful magazine editor, feature writer, newspaper reporter, drama critic, and author of widely anthologized short stories. She has taught writing in both high school and college, and it was during her tenure at the University of Oregon that this book had its genesis.

Reference Guides from MENTOR and SIGNET

The Lively Art of Writing

By Lucile Vaughan Payne

A MENTOR BOOK from
NEW AMERICAN LIBRARY
TIMES MIRROR
New York and Scarborough, Ontario

MENTOR TRADEMARK REG. U.S. PAT. OFF. AND FOREIGN COUNTRIES
REGISTERED TRADEMARK—MARCA REGISTRADA
HECHO EN CHICAGO, U.S.A.

SIGNET, SIGNET CLASSICS, MENTOR, PLUME, MERIDIAN AND NAL BOOKS are published *in the United States* by
The New American Library, Inc.,
1633 Broadway, New York, New York 10019,
in Canada by The New American Library of Canada Limited,
81 Mack Avenue, Scarborough, Ontario M1L 1M8

First Mentor Printing, March, 1969

13   14   15   16   17   18

PRINTED IN THE UNITED STATES OF AMERICA

Acknowledgments

I would like to acknowledge first my debt to all my former students. I had been writing a good many years before I ever tried to teach writing, so I had to learn about teaching it mostly by trial and error, by finding out from the students themselves what their problems were, what would work and what wouldn't work. They bore with me with patience and good humor, and they taught me a great deal. Most of the material in this book grew out of our mutual efforts to understand each other.

For the book's general organization and for the idea behind the section called "How to Write Badly by Trying Very, Very Hard" I owe a debt to Sheridan Baker's *The Practical Stylist* (Crowell, 1962), and I am grateful to Mr. Baker personally for his generous encouragement of my own efforts.

Finally, I want to express my gratitude to Miss Jeannette Elder and Mr. Robert E. Allen of the Follett Publishing Company: to Miss Elder for her wise and tireless editorial assistance, and to Mr. Allen for the adventurous spirit that led him to place this enterprise in my hands in the first place and to give me free rein in developing it.

Contents

A Note to the Student

This book has one purpose: to help you improve your writing style.

Style, if it can be summed up in a sentence, is the ability to say in writing, with clarity and economy and grace, precisely what you want to say. It sounds quite simple, put that way. But of course it is not simple at all. And it is not an easy thing to learn.

But it has certain basic elements that can be learned, and this book is designed to help you learn them. It points out some things to do when you write—and some things not to do. It explains and demonstrates specific techniques and provides exercises that will help you master them. It will probably clarify for you a great many things about writing that you have never quite understood before.

All your work will be with the essay, for it is the most versatile and the most useful of all the prose forms for the student of writing. You will begin by finding out exactly what it is and how it is put together. Then you will learn how to organize your own thoughts in the same way, around one central point. And you will start writing, immediately.

You will write first the whole essay, in order to get a full sense of its structure. But with each chapter you will move deeper and deeper into the essay, studying progressively smaller parts of it, writing as you go, making new discoveries about style as you write.

You will write paragraphs, finding out exactly how they are made, getting the feel of them, learning their relationships to each other. And then you will learn the many and marvelous things that can be done with sentences and with the words that go into them. You will experiment with the subtle skills of metaphor and simile, of allusion, of tone. And you will go on to new adventures with different kinds of essays.

By the time you have finished this book, you should have learned enough about style to improve your writing more than you ever believed possible. Now is the time to begin.

1

handwritten: Object of writing is to: communicate

What Is an Essay?

Ever since the first caveman discovered that he could draw arrows on the ground with a pointed stick, or scratch designs on the walls of his cave with a piece of flint, man has been trying to communicate with other men by means of written symbols. The caveman's arrows may have served only to show other cavemen the location of a river or the direction taken by an unfriendly animal. The designs he etched on the stone walls of his parlor may have represented no more than an instinctive effort at self-expression. But whatever his motives, that distant ancestor of ours was responding to a basic human urge—the urge to communicate. And although writing today is far more complicated, more subtle, more conscious in its purpose than were those first crude symbols of early man, the basic urge behind every piece of writing remains the same: to communicate, to share knowledge and ideas and feelings, to say to the world, "This is the way things are."

That is the purpose of all writing. It is the purpose of a newspaper report, of a magazine article, of a short story, of a novel, of a poem. And it is the purpose of the essay.

An essay, however, is neither a mere record of fact nor a pure work of the imagination. The paper that you write for a history class, crowded with facts you have gathered from reference works, may look like an essay. But it probably isn't, no matter how carefully you have rewritten all the facts in your own words. Neither is the autobiographical incident that you "write up" for your English class likely to be an essay, no matter how truthful or clever; nor the painstaking, step-by-step "How to . . ." paper, no matter how clear and precise; nor the description of a particular scene, no matter how accurate the details or how lyrical the language.

You have probably written hundreds of such compositions during your life, lumping them all together under that much-abused heading, "themes." You may even have called them essays. But they are seldom essays.

What, then, is an essay?

An essay is the written expression of its author's opinion.

handwritten: Express ophion & support it. Purpose is not to prove, but to persuade.

At its best an essay blends fact with imagination, knowledge with feeling, never giving itself over wholly to one or the other. But its purpose is always the same: to express an opinion. Essays will differ in quality and in kind, in length, in style, in subject. They will range from the very simple to the exceedingly complex. But in the final analysis every essay expresses a personal opinion. This is the critical difference between the essay and the expository theme or the mere report. An essay does not merely record facts or recount experiences; it registers the author's *opinion* of these facts and experiences.

That is why its study is so rewarding. Too often students let themselves become machines, ingesting the information their teachers offer them and then feeding it back, like ticker tape, in the form of rote recitations and answers to examination questions. But a student is no machine when he writes an essay; he is a human being—judging, evaluating, interpreting, expressing not only what he knows but what he *is*. Thus every attempted essay is a kind of voyage toward self-discovery.

The methods an essayist may use to express his opinion vary enormously, depending to some extent upon subject matter but to an even greater extent upon the author's particular view of life, his way of looking at things. He may put his opinion forward seriously or humorously, scientifically or imaginatively, formally or informally. He may state it explicitly, or he may imply it subtly. But opinion is always present. It is at the heart of every essay.

Obviously, then, you must have an opinion before you can write an essay. Therefore you need to know exactly what an opinion is, how to arrive at it, how to judge its value. Before you can reach an opinion, however, you must decide upon a subject, for no opinion exists in a vacuum. It always exists in relation to a particular subject. So we begin our search for opinion with the question, "What makes a good subject?"

Subjects for Essays

1) experiences
2) specialized knowlege

"What shall I write about?" This is the universal student question, a kind of midnight howl of anguish, loudest and most hopeless the night before an essay assignment is due. Yet of all the problems an essayist must tackle, the choice of subject is in some ways the simplest. For the choice is almost limitless. You can write an essay about literally anything—friendship or fashions, Puritanism or politics, shoes or ships or sealing wax. You can even write an essay about essays. Anything that the human mind has ever considered or investigated or wondered about provides material for an essay.

The only requirement is that the writer know enough about his subject to arrive at some kind of opinion.

What constitutes "knowing enough"? Certainly some ideas and experiences are so familiar to all of us that it can be safely said that everybody "knows enough." These are the commonplaces of human existence—friendship, family relationships, growing up, eating and sleeping, working and playing. The list is almost endless; it is simply the stuff of everyday life. And it provides an immense body of material for essays, all of it immediately and equally available to any writer.

"Knowing enough" to write about some subjects, however, requires familiarity with more specialized knowledge. An essay on Puritanism, for example—or a foreign language or internal-combustion engines or sailboating or microbiology— would be meaningless unless its author had a knowledge of his subject beyond the mere accidental contact of everyday life. Every student knows a little about Puritanism, if only that Puritans wore tall black hats and took a rather dim view of sin. But Puritanism is an idea with a specific place in history, an idea that has had enormous significance in shaping our society. To write about it without adequate information or understanding would be to invite ridicule. It is possible to write an adequate essay on a topic like friendship without being in command of a large body of facts, but it is not possible to do so on a topic like Puritanism. This, or any other specialized subject, requires solid information.

Fortunately, such information is easily and quickly available. The reference shelves of the library brim with facts and expert opinion about everything under the sun. You can find out about literally anything that interests you; your own interests, in fact, will guide you faster than anything else toward a suitable essay topic. Even a mild interest has a way of taking fire when you give it the fuel of facts. And once you start reading, you will soon be in command of enough information to question, to compare, to make judgments of your own. By reading what others have already written about a subject that interests you, you will come very quickly into possession of specialized knowledge.

As a matter of fact, it's likely that you already have far more specialized knowledge at your fingertips than you realize. Since your first day of school you have been exposed to subject matter. Inevitably, you have opinions about it. Any subject listed on your transcript—particularly any subject that has awakened in you a real interest, or even a real antagonism —provides you with essay material. The subject may be as academic as Latin or as practical as auto mechanics: if you have studied it, you will almost certainly "know enough" to write an essay based on what you have learned.

Hobbies provide another rich source of specialized knowledge. The boy who likes to rebuild old cars, the girl who raises tropical fish, the enthusiastic jazz buff, the amateur photographer, the fly fisherman, the rockhound—all these hobbyists will assuredly "know enough" about their subjects to write about them with authority. The true hobbyist always has a solid body of information about his special interest. And he has plenty of ideas about it—ideas that he is prepared to explain and defend with confidence. Or indeed with passion. (Have you ever heard two boys arguing the merits of double overhead cams? Or a devotee of progressive jazz in altercation with a disciple of Dixieland?) Both parties in such disputes are equipped with plenty of information and experience to back up their opinions.

And that, incidentally, tends to make the essay based on specialized knowledge much easier to write than the essay based on a familiar idea or commonplace experience. The author's opinion is an *informed* opinion. To put it bluntly, he knows what he's talking about. What passes for opinion in relation to familiar ideas and experiences, however, is all too often merely prejudice or habit or some fuzzy generalization that the author "feels" to be true. But as an essayist you cannot rely on mere feeling. You must dig through all sorts of vague impressions and obscure convictions in order to isolate a real opinion—a firmly held, specific, reasonable statement of what you *think* rather than a foggy declaration of what you feel.

But regardless of the kind of essay you choose to write— whether it is based primarily on knowledge or primarily on experience—you must have an *opinion* about your subject. What you know about it is important. What you feel about it is important. But more important than either is your opinion of what you know or feel. That is where your essay must begin.

wt some-1 thinks aBt ive in own mind

What Is an Opinion, and How Do You Reach It?

Most of us use the word "opinion" very loosely. We tend to claim as opinions all sorts of prejudices, sentiments, platitudes, and vague convictions. But a genuine opinion, strong enough

fact - proven -- based on absolute certainty

to support the structure of an essay, must meet certain specifications, all of them clearly laid out in this definition:

> opinion: A belief not based on absolute certainty or positive knowledge but on what seems true, valid, or probable to one's own mind; what one thinks; judgment.

You could not find a tool better suited to your purposes than this definition. Test any opinion against it and you will know immediately whether you have chosen a valid essay topic. It will make clear the difference between opinion and fact; the failure to make this distinction is perhaps the commonest error among student writers.

Is your opinion based on absolute certainty? On positive knowledge? Can you prove beyond all reasonable doubt that it is true? Then it is not an opinion at all. It is a fact—or an observation so commonplace that it has the status of fact.

Facts must be converted into opinions before they can serve as essay topics. It is a fact, for example, that the population of the United States is now more than 200 million. The figure is a matter of record; it can be proved. To convert such a fact into a suitable essay topic you must ask yourself what it means; you must *judge* it, reach an opinion about it. Your judgment might be that the character of our national life is changing as a result of our increased population; or that immediate research is necessary to guarantee a food supply in the future; or that new ways of educating young people must be found if public education is to survive. Thus, by making a judgment, you have converted a fact into an opinion—and you have a valid essay topic.

Sometimes an opinion must be discarded as an essay topic because it is so generally accepted that it has the status of fact. Suppose, for example, that you choose to write an essay about friendship. You may come up with an opinion like this: "Friendship is an important human relationship." Fact or opinion? You may claim it is opinion because it cannot be scientifically or statistically proved. Yet it is a poor opinion for essay purposes because it is not in any real sense subject to argument. For all practical purposes, it is a fact. Only an extremely gifted and original writer could hope to make it interesting. In the hands of a beginner such a commonplace is almost certain to be overpoweringly dull.

Opinions in this category must be converted, as facts must be converted, into sharply defined judgments. Merely by changing the statement to "Friendship is *the most important* human relationship" you add a little zest to your topic. But the best way to convert a commonplace into an interesting, thought-provoking essay topic is to bombard it with questions: Do boys make better friends than girls? Is real friendship possible between a boy and a girl? Between parents and their children? Does friendship usually have an element of self-interest? Your answer to any one of these questions (or to a hundred others that may occur to you) will provide you, automatically, with an *opinion*—and therefore an essay topic.

You will notice that an answer to any of the questions above will commit you to an opinion because the answer in each case is simply "yes" or "no." This is perhaps the simplest method of arriving at an opinion. But you may find an even more interesting essay topic by asking yourself "how, why, and what" questions:

How can parents and children learn to be friends?
Why are boys better friends than girls (or vice versa)?
What is friendship?

These are all questions that require a complete statement as an answer. They are, as a matter of fact, the same questions you are likely to ask yourself as you develop an essay from the simple "yes or no" answer that may get you started. The point is that in either case the answer is an *opinion*.

The more questions you ask yourself, the better. Questions force you down from a great cloudy mass of ideas to the solid ground of real thought. You will learn quickly to recognize the questions that are pointless, or that require too much information, or that simply can't be answered in the brief space of an essay. And you will discover, as you formulate and answer questions, a great many opinions you have never before put into words—which is another way of saying that you had never really known what you really think. Don't snatch the first answer that occurs to you and call off the search. Keep asking questions. When you come up with an answer so interesting and challenging that it strikes you as a personal discovery, you can be sure you have moved into the true essayist's territory.

The same process applies to more academic subjects. Your first thought about Puritanism, for example, might be that "Puritanism was a strong influence on early American society." But this is not opinion. It is fact. You can prove it without the slightest difficulty. Therefore it is a poor essay topic. Bombard it with questions that can be answered with *opinions*, and you begin collecting good essay topics: Is Puritanism dead, or is it still an active force in American life? Can it

to change fact to opinion -- ask quest's -- how, why, etc.

Is there opposition! Are there facts to support

WHAT IS AN ESSAY? 19

explain some of our attitudes today? How? What was wrong with the Puritan definition of religious freedom? As questions and answers multiply, your problem is no longer one of finding an essay topic but of choosing the most interesting one among many.

What Makes an Opinion Interesting? _someone else disagrees_ OPPOSITION

You will quickly discover that certain opinions you reach seem more interesting than others. Certainly your own enthusiasm for your subject has something to do with this. All of us write best about the subjects we like best. Or you may find one topic more interesting than another simply because you have done a better job of putting it into words; some happy turn of phrase has given it spice and character. But more effective than anything else in arousing interest in an opinion is _opposition:_ if a substantial number of people disagree with your views on a subject, you may be sure that your views will excite interest.

This is the real explanation for the weakness of a topic like "Friendship is important." It falls flat because nobody of reasonable intelligence would dream of challenging it. Readers simply are not interested in an opinion so obviously and demonstrably true. You could write some kind of paper about it, of course, but who would want to read it? Your mother, maybe. Or your best friend. But even they might have difficulty disguising their yawns.

No argument, no essay. It is almost as simple as that. For every essay, in the final analysis, is an argument. It is an author pitting his opinion against every other opinion on the same subject. The stronger the opposition, the hotter the argument—and the greater the interest. Make certain, therefore, when you choose an opinion to defend, that it is an opinion that rubs at least a few people the wrong way. "Girls are smarter than boys"—say that (if you're bold enough) and immediately you have about half the population opposing you. "Boys are smarter than girls"—say that (if you're bolder still) and you have the other half on your back. Opposition— and therefore interest—is guaranteed.

Value judgments of the "this-is-better-than-that" variety always have a clear-cut opposition. But it is not really necessary to be so bluntly argumentative. Often you need only take a position. For example, the moment you say "Drag racing promotes safety," you are arguing against the opinion of all the people who think it promotes nothing but trouble. "Stu-

No argument—No essay

dents should be required to do more writing" will almost certainly outrage students who consider the creation of even one sentence a labor beyond endurance. Say that "The best movie of the year was *The Purple Monster*," and you will draw the immediate fire of the movie-goer who is certain that the best movie of the year was *The Polka Dot Monster*. Even a difference in interpretation can provide the necessary element of controversy: "*The Purple Monster* gave an accurate portrayal of the typical American housewife" will stir up everybody who considered the movie a vicious attack on American womanhood.

Examining the Opposition

As you begin to shape opinions for essays, force yourself to question your position by considering carefully everything that can be said in favor of an exactly opposite opinion. If you want to prove that drag racing promotes safety, look for the reasons that other people have for believing that it promotes a love of danger. If you believe students should do *more* writing, consider all the reasons for doing *less* writing. Make yourself thoroughly aware of every argument that might be used against your particular point of view.

It is not always possible, of course, to find an opinion exactly opposite to your own. If you claim that *The Purple Monster* was the year's best movie, the exactly opposite claim would be that it was the year's worst movie. But maybe nobody makes this claim. Maybe the critics have simply failed to give the movie as much attention as you think it deserves; or maybe they have said only that it was too long or too short or too noisy. Or possibly too purple. Their opinions are not precisely the opposite of yours. They are merely different from yours. In that case, your job is to examine the arguments they use to support these opinions.

Such careful consideration of every side of an issue occasionally has the surprising result of causing you to change your mind. Splendid. You still have an opinion—merely a different one. And you are likely to be an even stronger advocate of your new opinion than you were of the old. But even if your first opinion is as strong as ever, your tour through opposition territory will have made you more aware of the strengths and weaknesses of your position, thus giving you a better idea of how to defend it.

An opinion, after all, is simply one person's idea of the truth, his guess at the meaning of facts or ideas or circumstances. Suppose a study of your town reveals that the crime rate has gone up in the past few years. X, after considering the facts, makes one judgment (the town has an inadequate police force); Y makes a different judgment (the churches or the schools are failing in their responsibilities); Z arrives at still another judgment (the town is in the hands of corrupt politicians). Each is able to defend his judgment with honest conviction, for it is his idea of the truth.

Which judgment is correct? Which represents the final truth? Nobody knows, for truth is not something that can be weighed, measured, labeled, and conveniently stored for future reference. But the public, after weighing the arguments of X, Y, and Z, will accept as truth the opinion that is supported by the most evidence, that is the most logical, the fairest, the most clearly stated, the most persuasive.

Even so with an essay. You cannot expect your opinion to be subject to scientific proof. Your purpose is to persuade, not to prove, and the strength of your essay will depend upon how well you persuade a reader to agree with your particular view. Every opinion that you are considering as a potential essay topic, then, should be checked against these questions:

1. Can a valid argument be made against it?
2. Can I defend it logically against this argument?

If you can answer "yes" to both these questions, you can be reasonably sure that you are on the trail of an interesting essay topic.

A gifted and original writer can, of course, present his ideas with such fresh insight and in such beguiling language that his essay will be interesting even without a clearly defined opposing point of view. He may simply want to arouse interest where none existed before. In that case, he must overcome the roughest opposition that a writer can face— pure apathy, the reluctance of most readers to bother with anything that doesn't rouse their instinct to take sides.

The beginner will find it easier, on the whole, to write his first essays on topics that have a clearly defined opposition.

Believe What You Say

A good essay topic will always be subject to argument. But the argument must be honest and intelligent. You can arouse temporary interest, of course, with an opinion that contradicts all logic or established facts (Friendship is unimportant, Puritanism had no influence). But a bizarre opinion manufactured simply to attract attention is an obvious and silly device. Worse yet, it's dishonest. You are naturally eager to escape dullness, but if you must make a choice between a dull topic and a dishonest one, by all means choose dullness. Dullness in writing can be cured. Dishonesty can't. An essay based on a dishonest opinion will always carry with it Big Daddy's "odor of mendacity," and nothing can disguise that particular smell. Honesty is quite literally the best policy for the essayist; it's the only policy, in fact, that works.

So believe in your opinion. This does not mean that you should reject summarily every opinion that doesn't get your immediate and wholehearted approval. To the contrary. Ideas that don't get your immediate approval are the very ones you should look at most closely. You cannot, after all, claim to have arrived at an opinion until you have examined, thoroughly and fairly, every legitimate argument against it. But once you have done this, you can be secure in your belief, and it will help guide you between the Scylla of dullness and the Charybdis of mendacity.

Summary

Pick a subject, examine everything you know about it, arrive at an honest opinion. That probably sounds easy. It isn't. But it represents at least half the work involved in writing an essay. And most of it you can do without touching a pencil. The first axiom of the essayist could hardly be made clearer:

Think before you write.

In other words, never sit down to write until you have thought long enough and hard enough about one subject to have an opinion about it—an opinion that you believe in and want to share, one that you can defend logically and honestly. Most writing skills are relatively easy to learn, but it is pointless to learn them—in fact, you will find it almost impossible to learn them—unless you have learned the first rule, the unbreakable rule, of essay writing:

Opinion always comes first.

And of course it comes first because, as soon as you have an opinion, you have something to say. That's the important thing: have something to say. Then you can learn how to say it. The skills come easily when you have a purpose for learning them. Have something to say—and if you really want to be heard, nothing can stop you from learning how to say it well.

Questions

1. What is the difference between opinion and fact?
2. How important are facts in an essay?
3. Is one opinion as good as another? Explain your answer.
4. Assuming that the writer has an adequate background in his subject, would American foreign policy be a good general subject for an essay? Why or why not?
5. The titles below are grouped around particular subjects. Which title in each group would make the best essay topic? Why?

   a. Sewing as a Hobby
   b. Clothes You Make Yourself
   c. Sewing Is Suddenly "In"
   d. How to Make a Pleated Skirt

   e. Cars for Teen-Agers
   f. Driver-Training Programs Cost Too Much
   g. Twin Carburetors
   h. Styling on the Latest Sports Models

   i. *Moby Dick*
   j. The Symbolism in *Moby Dick*
   k. The Character of Ahab in *Moby Dick*
   l. *Moby Dick*, America's Greatest Novel

   m. Why Should Students Study Literature?
   n. High Points in American Literature
   o. Literature in Relation to History
   p. Most Students Can't Read

   q. The Student Council Is Outmoded
   r. Student Councils and Student Government
   s. The President of the Student Council
   t. Your Student Council

6. What is the chief difference between a typical term paper and an essay?

7. What is the weakness of each of the following essay topics?

   a. Edison Invented the Electric-Light Bulb
   b. Teachers Should Explain Things Clearly
   c. Science Has Influenced Modern Life
   d. Safe Driving Should Be Encouraged
   e. The Responsibilities of Students

ASSIGNMENT

1. Write a one-sentence opinion based on each of the subjects below:

laughter	apples	drag racing
art	grades	popularity
fear	fashions	shoes

2. Choose one of your opinions, and list at least three facts that will support it.
3. Write a one-sentence opinion that is exactly opposite to yours, and list three facts that will support it. (You may not agree with the opinion, but you must use convincing facts.)
4. Write at least two paragraphs using *all* the material you have written for #2 and #3 (the two opinions and both sets of facts). You must reword the material to suit your purpose, but be sure to use all of it in some way, relating the paragraphs clearly so that the reader will understand why you favor one opinion instead of the other.

VOCABULARY

1. Look up the following words in a dictionary. Find a synonym and an antonym for each word. List them under separate headings marked *Words—Synonyms—Antonyms*.

adequate	antagonism	platitude
altercation	apathy	valid

2. In your opinion, what is the meaning of the term "value judgment"? Use a specific example to illustrate.
3. In the chapter you have just read, the following two phrases appear: "the odor of mendacity" and "the Scylla of dullness and the Charybdis of mendacity." Look up the meanings of *mendacity, Scylla,* and *Charybdis.* Find the text sentences containing these phrases, and copy the complete sentences. Then, in your own words, explain exactly what the sentences mean.

2
From Opinion to Thesis

In Chapter 1, the word "opinion" appeared over and over. The repetition was deliberate. Its purpose was to impress permanently upon your mind the need to have an opinion on your subject before you begin to write an essay.

Now it is time to take a closer look at that word "opinion." It's a rather broad term. When you say, "It looks like rain," you are expressing an opinion—but it is not an opinion likely to inspire an essay. As a budding essayist, you need a word that more precisely describes the particular kind of opinion represented in an essay.

That word is *thesis*.

> *The thesis of your essay is your opinion boiled down to one arguable statement.*

Everything else in the essay depends on your thesis, for the whole purpose of your essay is to explain and clarify and defend and illustrate it—and thus to persuade the reader of its truth. The thesis is, you might say, pure extract of essay; it is the *one major point* you want to make, with everything else stripped away. It is a straight unadorned statement of the opinion you have chosen as your essay topic. You arrive at this opinion through a process of selection that is the very essence of thought—the narrowing of a broad subject to one specific judgment.

You have already had a glimpse of this process with topics like *friendship* and *Puritanism* in Chapter 1. You know generally that what you must do is to pick your way through a great mass of ideas and impressions and finally to "close in" on your subject. Now let's watch the process at work.

"Closing In" on Your Thesis

No hard and fast rule can cover all the methods of "closing in." Too much depends upon the kind of subject you have chosen and upon your own way of thinking about things. But certain general principles can guide you, as you will see in the examples that follow.

Let's assume that you have been asked to work out a thesis based on one of the subjects below:

drag racing	silverware
slang	magazines
hair styles	furniture

The topics have been roughly divided according to type. *Drag racing, slang,* and *hair styles* represent subjects that are familiar to you: you probably know quite a bit about at least one of the three, either through experience or through observation. An informal essay on the one you know best would probably not present too great a challenge.

The second group of subjects is a little more formidable. Here are simply the names of concrete objects. They are ordinary enough, but they are less directly related to your immediate concerns and probably do not interest you very much. Of the three, *silverware* is likely to draw the biggest blank in your mind. It seems reasonable to assume, therefore, that if you can formulate a thesis on silverware, a relatively unfamiliar subject of scant interest, you should be able to handle any familiar and more interesting subject with still happier results. So let's start with silverware, just to get the feel of things.

The Five-Step Process

The process of finding a thesis is mainly a process of finding out, first, what you know about a subject and then determining what your opinion is of what you know. It can be reduced to five basic steps:

1. Take inventory.

Since finding a thesis is a process of narrowing your subject to one specific idea—one opinion—you must first take inventory of all you know about silverware. So how much do you know about it? Pitifully little, probably, unless you have an uncle in the business, or in the unlikely event that silverware is your secret passion. But you can't say you know *nothing* about it. You know what it is, what it looks like, how it feels in your hand. And undoubtedly you can summon up stray observations you have made and bits of information you have heard. What these bits and pieces are depends upon your own experience, of course. Just be certain that you have in mind absolutely everything you know about silverware.

2. Ask questions.

Look over your inventory and ask yourself questions. You might come up with something like this:

> A. I wonder why some silverware is heavier than other silverware.
> B. What's the meaning of the expression, "born with a silver spoon in his mouth"?
> C. Why do so many women want to own sterling silver?

Already you have enough questions to get started toward a thesis. Question A you would discard rather quickly, for it can be answered with facts. And you are looking for opinion, not fact. Question B can also be answered rather easily, but the answer itself may contain the germ of a thesis. A man "born with a silver spoon in his mouth" is, of course, a man born into a rich and probably indulgent family. Are his chances for success greater than ordinary? Certainly your answer to this question will be an opinion. Perhaps you have stumbled onto a thesis.

But wait a minute. It may be a thesis, but is it really about the topic assigned? It is not. Your mental processes have led you to switch from an essay on silverware to an essay on the advantages or disadvantages of inherited wealth. Go back again to your questions. Move on to Question C. Maybe it will guide you to a thesis.

3. Look for relationships.

Why do so many women want to own sterling silver? Your first quick answer might be simply that most women love beautiful things. But look closely at this answer. Certainly most women love beautiful things, but how do you explain the fact that many women apparently love beautiful silver more than they love beautiful sculpture or painting or music or even beautiful buttons? Sterling silver costs a great deal of money. With the same amount of money a woman could buy a great many beautiful things besides silver. But she chooses to buy silver. She may even make real sacrifices to buy it.

Now you are beginning to "close" with your subject, to demand more than the first easy answer that occurs to you.

That old quotation wanders back into your mind: "born with a silver spoon in his mouth." Could a woman's desire to own silver be related to that? Suddenly you make a connection: *Maybe owning sterling silver makes a woman feel rich.* It seems to make sense. Obviously we tend to connect silver with riches. That silver spoon probably came down to us from an era when only kings and queens and noblemen could afford to own real silver. So silver is a symbol of wealth, security, superiority.

4. Ask the yes-or-no question.

Can it be that silverware is a status symbol? Answer your own question with a yes or no:

Thesis A: Sterling silver is a status symbol.
Thesis B: Sterling silver is not a status symbol.

You are on the right track. But by taking either thesis as it stands, you put yourself in the inflexible position of arguing that sterling silver is *always* a status symbol or that it is *never* a status symbol. And no matter which position you take, you must be able to defend it. That, after all, is the whole purpose of your essay—to defend your thesis. Now you are uneasily aware that a rigid either/or position would be almost impossible to defend. So you must take one more step.

5. Qualify.

Qualification is simply the process of limiting your thesis to exactly the area you choose to defend, thus making your point of view precise and reasonable. Since you cannot possibly prove that sterling silver is always a status symbol, nor that it is never a status symbol, you must indicate the *degree* of truth in your thesis and, if possible, the circumstances under which you are considering it. Thus you emerge finally with something like this:

Thesis A: Many women own sterling silver because they think of it as an important status symbol.
Thesis B: Many women want to own sterling silver because it symbolizes both stability and beauty in family life.

Note that Thesis B is now affirmative rather than negative. The word "not" is always weakening in a thesis. You should always tell your reader what *is*, rather than what is *not*.

Now you know exactly what it is that you are going to explain and defend. Your arguments might run something like this:

Thesis A: The average housewife seldom uses her sterling silver; even though she claims that she wants it because it is beautiful, she does not use it to beautify her daily life.

The more expensive it is, the better she likes it. Its cost is more important to her than its design.

She "shows it off" exactly as her husband "shows off" his expensive new car—to impress their friends.

Thesis B: The average housewife needs to surround herself with as many beautiful things as possible. Otherwise she is likely to find her life drab and meaningless.

If her only interest were status, she could buy goldplate or some of the new and even more expensive metals.

Far from being a mere status symbol, sterling silver is an intimate and enduring symbol of basic family relationships.

The argument, as you can see, is just about equally strong on either side. You may be convinced first by one, then by the other. And that is exactly as it should be. *After having considered both sides,* you will settle eventually on the view that seems to you to be closest to the truth. You cannot, after all, claim to have arrived at a valid judgment on any question until you have examined all the arguments that can be used against you.

So always look very closely and objectively at views opposed to your own. If you do this, you may be forced to concede a point here and there, to qualify your thesis a little more strictly—but this merely leads to greater accuracy in presenting your own view. And then you are in a stronger position than ever to write your essay. You can defend your thesis with real conviction.

A Subject Close to Home

We began our discussion of finding a thesis with *silverware* because it looked so unpromising as a subject. Now let's take a look at a subject that should be easier because it is a lively part of everyday life for many young people and because it has an almost built-in element of controversy: *drag racing.* Nearly everybody has an opinion about drag racing; one tends to be either violently for it or violently against it. Such violence always indicates high emotional voltage—and high interest value. But the emotion must be brought under control. Watch the thesis statements below as they progress gradually, on both sides of the question, from mere generalized emotion to reasonable, specific opinion that can be defended:

A. Drag racing is wonderful.
B. Drag racing is terrible.
    (*All emotion; no appeal to reason.*)

A. Drag racing is the perfect sport for today's youth.
B. Drag racing is a senseless and dangerous pastime.
    (*Overstatement; still too much emotion.*)

A. Drag racing is one of the best of all sports for today's youth.
B. Drag racing is little more than a senseless and dangerous pastime.
    (*Somewhat qualified, but still too general—what does "best" mean?*)

A. Drag racing is an excellent way to develop skilled mechanics as well as good drivers.
B. Drag racing encourages boys to waste time and money and to endanger their lives in senseless speed.
    (*Better; more specific, but a bit flat.*)

A. Today's drag-racing teen-ager is primarily an automotive engineer, as eager to test his theories as to win races.
B. Today's drag-racing teen-ager is usually an irresponsible show-off whose ignorant love for speed makes him a public menace.
    (*Final thesis; reasonable, specific opinion that can be defended.*)

Notice that as the thesis sentences change, they change in only one major respect: *They become more accurate.* The writer's opinion of drag racing in the final version of Thesis A, for example, is basically no different from the opinion he expresses in his first version—quite obviously he still approves of drag racing. And in the final Thesis B he still obviously disapproves of it. But the sweeping generalizations of "wonderful" and "terrible" have given way, in each thesis, to a very specific statement that points toward a reasonable and informed discussion rather than a mere expression of prejudice. Furthermore, the writer still has plenty of room under

side I choose
I defend

either final thesis to bring up any of the points he might have brought up under the first version. If he uses Thesis A, he will emphasize mechanical skill, but he will undoubtedly use such related points as pride in workmanship, quick reflexes, respect for rules. If he uses the negative thesis (or *antithesis*✱) he will, of course, emphasize the evils inherent in the obsession with speed, and pull in as related points all his other objections to drag racing. Increased accuracy in a thesis does not necessarily limit argument; it simply improves organization.

Accuracy in a thesis results, primarily, from qualification. To say that drag racing is the "perfect" sport is to make far too sweeping a claim. But to qualify that claim slightly, to say not that it is perfect (nothing is perfect), but that it is "one of the best" is to move a little closer to the truth. Each succeeding statement moves still closer. Only the most impassioned drag racer would try to defend his hobby as the *perfect* sport; and if he is as hardheaded and impassioned as all that, he is not likely to have anything very reasonable to say about drag racing—or about anything else.

By the same token, the writer who states flatly, without qualification, that drag racing is *nothing but* a senseless and dangerous pastime has lost his claim to reasonableness. A very large body of opinion disagrees with this particular judgment; if the writer has examined all the evidence, he must admit that drag racing probably has a few points in its favor. So he qualifies: *nothing but* becomes *little more than*. And immediately he is on far safer ground. He has notified the reader that he has looked at both sides of the question, as a reasonable man should, and that he is not speaking from blind prejudice.

Summary

Every essay is an opinion, but not every opinion is a good essay topic. It is a good topic only if it can be boiled down to one arguable statement about one major point. This statement is called a thesis, and you arrive at it by a process of thinking that has five steps: first, by taking inventory of your information; second, by asking yourself general questions, or "wondering" about your material; third, by relating it to your general information and experience; fourth, by asking the

✱ *Antithesis* is a word you should know. It means, literally, "against thesis," as you can probably guess by its prefix. But the pronunciation is tricky. The accent falls on the second syllable, and that "i" is short: an-tith′ə-sis.

yes-or-no question; and fifth, by qualifying your answer to this question.

That qualified answer is your thesis. You know now precisely what it is you want to say—and that is the first long step in the path toward better writing.

QUESTIONS

1. What is the difference between opinion and thesis?
2. What is the five-step process for narrowing a general subject to a thesis?
3. What is the value of the yes-or-no question?
4. Why is qualification of a thesis important?

ASSIGNMENT

At the top of a sheet of paper, write the name of some subject in which you are now enrolled. Then do the following:

1. Write at least five statements of fact about it.
2. Write at least two yes-or-no questions that occur to you in relation to these facts.
3. Write a thesis based on one of the questions.
4. Write an antithesis. (If your antithesis is not valid, write a new thesis. Keep trying until you are sure that both thesis and antithesis can be defended.)
5. Give at least one reason (or one piece of evidence) supporting your antithesis.
6. Give at least two reasons (or pieces of evidence) supporting your thesis.
7. Write a paragraph based on your thesis (#3). Include in this paragraph the point supporting the antithesis (#5) and both the points supporting your thesis (#6). Bear in mind that your purpose is to persuade a reader to agree with your thesis. Organize your paragraph in the way that seems to be best for this purpose.

VOCABULARY

1. Find a synonym to use in place of each of the italicized words in the sentences below. Rewrite the sentences if necessary.

    a. Everything he had to say on the subject was the *antith-esis* of all I believed.

    b. He is so *arbitrary* in his judgments that it is impossible to reason with him.

    c. Nobody believes that point is *arguable*.

    d. He was a small, meek-looking man, but he was a *formidable* opponent in a debate.

    e. His *impassioned* plea fell on deaf ears.

    f. He was an *indulgent* grandfather.

    g. Nobody ever had a more *unpromising* start in business.

2. The words "principle" and "principal" are often confused because they sound alike although they are spelled differently and have different meanings. Sometimes the only way to master such words is to invent some private trick—a rhyme, a joke, any kind of nonsense that will help you remember their difference. It doesn't matter how silly it seems, if it works. One student, for example, wrote "I can remember that 'principle' means 'rule' because it ends like 'disciple' which reminds me of the Golden Rule." It worked for him. What works for you? Write two or three sentences explaining how you keep these words and their spelling (and meaning) clear in your own mind. If you don't already have a trick of your own, make one up.

3. Write a sentence or two defining "status symbol" and giving a specific example of some kind of status symbol that a student might use. (Don't use an automobile as your example. Make it a status symbol that the student could wear or carry with him.)

3

The Full and Final Thesis

In learning how to arrive at a thesis you have already taken the first major step in improving your skill in writing essays. The next step is the preparation of a full thesis statement. This step may seem purely mechanical, and in a sense it is mechanical. You could learn to do it without ever knowing the processes it represents, just as you can turn an ignition key and start a motor without any understanding of the internal-combustion engine. Actually, your thesis is a kind of ignition key to your essay; until you turn it your writing will generate no power.

But beyond this point the analogy breaks down. Ideas and engines are very different things. You can drive a thousand miles without understanding the principles of internal combustion, but you will not take a very long or very interesting trip in an essay unless you understand not only how to prepare a full thesis but why you do it. That *why* is very important.

First, however, you need to know exactly what is meant by full thesis.

Elements of a Full Thesis

So far, your thesis is simply your opinion sharpened to one pointed statement. Your *full thesis* will have three elements:

1. Thesis
2. Points that can be made against your thesis
3. Points in favor of your thesis

Putting these three elements together in a full thesis statement requires no particular writing skill; at this point you are not concerned with stylistic flourishes. You are merely arranging, in an orderly way, the raw materials you will be working with when you write. The full thesis statement never appears in its original form in the finished essay. But its importance can hardly be overestimated. For the full thesis is your only sure guide through the tangle of ideas that always surround an essay topic as soon as you begin to write in earnest.

The Psychology of Argument

The three elements of a full thesis represent the psychology of all argument, whether written or oral. The goal in any argument is identical to the goal in any essay—to win others to a particular point of view, to *persuade*. And the same three elements are always present in a successful argument, no matter whether it is a written essay, a formal debate, or even a family quarrel.

Suppose yourself in the midst of a typical family crisis. You want to borrow your father's car to take your girl to a dance. The last time you drove the car, however, you dented a fender

—a circumstance that causes your father to view any further driving on your part with something less than sympathy. How do you persuade him to let you use the car again?

If you are a man of few words and very little wisdom, you stride up to him, announce without preamble that you want the car, and wait to see what happens. Your father, if he is typical, will probably ask you if you have lost your mind. He may even shout a little, and wave his arms, and turn slightly purple.

Result: you don't get the car.

If you are a man of much emotion and little reason, you may use pressure tactics: "Gee whiz, Dad, I'm not ten years old, after all. Other guys my age drive all the time. I dent one crummy fender and you act like I committed a crime. Good grief, you ought to know I didn't do it on purpose. Anyway, it seems to me like you'd want to do something nice for me once in a while . . ." And so forth.

Sounds pretty adolescent, doesn't it? As certainly it is. Sincere, yes. Reasonable, no. It is simply a great incoherent jumble of injured emotionalism, and it will convince no parent that you are a mature and responsible person.

Result: you don't get the car.

So, if you are wise, you use a third approach. First of all, you modify that belligerent "I want the car!" It becomes a request rather than a demand: "I hope you'll consider letting me use the car tonight, Dad." Thus you recognize, by a process very similar to the process of qualifying a thesis, that the matter must be settled not merely on the basis of your private desires but on the basis of your father's authority. And your father, if he is a reasonable man, will be willing to hear you out. You are not groveling, but you are showing respect for his rights. And he appreciates it.

Then you admit that your father has good reason to mistrust your driving skill: "Dad, I know I was to blame for denting that fender last week . . ." Your father is agreeably impressed by the good sense of this remark. He is willing to go on listening. Nothing softens the opposition so much as a graceful admission that it has some points in its favor.

And so you wind up your case with the arguments most likely to work in your favor: "I made the date before I damaged the fender. Incidentally, I've already made arrangements to have it repaired and to pay for it myself. And I'd like another chance to prove to you that you can trust me to drive."

Result: you *may* get the car.

Your father, if he is a reasonable man, will at least be willing to consider your request fairly. And that is all, really, that you have the right to expect. But you have earned that right because you have presented your case as one reasonable man to another. You have not made a belligerent, unexplained demand ("I want the car!"), nor have you poured out an incoherent jumble of emotionalism ("I'm not ten years old . . . other guys . . . crummy fender . . . etc."). You have used, whether you know it or not, the psychology of argument. And it has a very definite pattern—a pattern identical to the one you will use in preparing a full thesis statement:

> 1. Thesis (accurate, qualified statement of main idea): "I hope you'll consider . . ."
> 2. Point that can be made against thesis: "I know I was to blame . . ."
> 3. Points in favor of thesis: "I made the date before . . .", "I'll pay for the damage . . .", "I'd like another chance to prove you can trust me . . ."

Strongest Argument Last

Observe that even in the arrangement of your reasons you follow a pattern. The reasons are presented in an ascending scale, with the strongest (from your father's point of view) coming last. The fact that you made the date before you damaged the fender is relatively unimportant to him; the fact that you have taken responsibility for the damage is much more important—he begins to feel some respect for you at this point; but most important of all to him is your desire to prove your trustworthiness, for it appeals both to his sense of fair play and to his instincts as a father. You need only to reverse the order of your reasons to see how your case would be weakened in your father's eyes.

Every successful argument, written or oral, conforms to the pattern: statement of case, recognition of opposition, and defense, with the strongest argument placed last. All this may make an essay seem no different from a debate or a trial by law. As a matter of fact, the underlying logic is identical. The difference is simply in emphasis, in language, and in style of execution. An essay may seem light as thistledown, intimate as a friendly conversation, but always at its core is the same inescapable iron logic of argument. The pattern may be beautifully disguised, but it will be there.

Form of the Full Thesis

Type or write your full thesis on a card or separate sheet of paper. Put it on the wall in front of your desk if possible; you should keep it in full view all the time you are working on your essay. The form is very simple. State your thesis and arrange your *pro* and *con* arguments below it. Your thesis on drag racing, for example, would look like this:

Thesis A: Today's drag-racing teen-ager is primarily an automotive engineer.

Con	Pro
Dangers of drag racing	Drivers become expert mechanics
Drivers irresponsible, merely attracted by danger	Pride in workmanship
Destructiveness (tire burning, etc.)	Respect for rules at dragstrips
Noisy, dirty	Most criticism uninformed
	Safety important

or

Thesis B: Today's drag-racing teen-ager is usually an ir-responsible show-off.

Con	Pro
Drivers are good mechanics	Wasteful, dirty, noisy
Pride in workmanship	Reckless love of danger
Respect for dragstrip rules	Emphasis on mechanical skill rather than on responsibility
	Racing instinct encouraged

Here, in a nutshell, is the substance of your entire essay for either thesis. The *con* arguments are placed on the left simply for convenience—you take care of these first. Then you can move on, developing fully the *pro* arguments that support your thesis.

Once you have this full thesis statement before you, a glance at it will tell you exactly what points you are going to make. Under *con* will be the points that can be made against your thesis; these you must be prepared to concede ("It is true that some young people are attracted to drag racing merely because of a reckless love of danger, but . . .") or to counter with reasonable argument ("Although most adults are quick to accuse drag racers of irresponsibility, few of them have any real knowledge of what goes on at a dragstrip . . ."). Think of your *con* list as the points you will *concede* and of your *pro* list as the points you will *propound,* and you will be on safe ground. Your *pro* list will always be the longer one, of course, for this is the main body of your argument.

Your paragraphs will not necessarily follow the exact order of the points listed in your full thesis. The points are there to *guide* you, remember, not to dictate to you. As you write you may find that their position in the essay needs to be shifted. A point that seemed minor may suddenly assume a new importance; one that at first seemed major may dwindle to relative insignificance. But all your carefully-thought-out ideas are there, ready for you to develop.

What if your thoughts suddenly branch out, expand, bring new ideas that seem important? By all means take advantage of their possibilities. Never let a good idea get away from you just because you didn't think of it before you wrote your full thesis statement. But always check out each new idea. Ask yourself: "Is it related to my main point? Does it make my point clearer or merely confuse it? Am I putting it where it belongs, or would it be more effective in another paragraph?" If a new idea works, if it will help persuade your reader, then by all means use it. No writer boxes himself in so rigidly with a full thesis statement that he can't wander afield to make a related point.

The full statement will, however, prevent you from wandering completely off course. If you continually check your developing essay against it, you won't find yourself discussing drag racing one minute and your pal Bill the next. You won't begin a paragraph on prom queens, bog down in a swamp of sentiment about misunderstood youth, and emerge ten sentences later with an observation on your Aunt Martha's chocolate pie. You will move freely around any point you wish to make, but you won't fly off in another direction altogether. Your full thesis is your check against the temptations of irrelevancy.

The temptations are strong. If your ideas come thick and fast when you write, you are tempted to grab them all and stuff them into your essay willy-nilly for fear of missing one good point. If your ideas come slowly and painfully, you are tempted to use anything that occurs to you in the hope that it will somehow miraculously fit. The full thesis guards you against either of these extremes. It disciplines the writer who has too many ideas, forcing him to organize his scattered thoughts and to check each one for relevance. It stimulates the writer who has too few ideas, reminding him of the exact points that he must bring out.

Summary

The full and final thesis is the thesis plus a list of the points that can be made against it and a longer list of the points in its favor. These *con* and *pro* points, listed separately for easy reference under the thesis, provide an organization chart for your entire essay. You should keep your full thesis statement on a separate card that is in full view all the time that you are writing. Use it, not as a rigid outline, but as a guide and a reminder. It will check your tendency to wander off course and will keep you constantly aware of the points you need to make.

The full thesis is a most remarkable and valuable device. Prepare it carefully, refer to it often, use it wisely. It will serve you well as you go more deeply into the structure of essays.

QUESTIONS

1. What are the three elements of a full thesis?
2. Explain the relationship of the full thesis to the psychology of argument.
3. Why should the full thesis statement be kept in view when you are writing an essay?
4. How strictly should you follow the full thesis when you write your essay?

ASSIGNMENT

1. Below are several thesis statements. Write a full thesis statement for each, using the form on page 37.

    a. The search for popularity generally leads to self-improvement.
    b. The search for popularity can limit a student's personal growth.
    c. All girls are slightly crazy.
    d. All boys are slightly crazy.
    e. Competition for grades is a healthy influence on students.
    f. Competition for grades is an unhealthy influence on students.

2. Using your full thesis statement as a guide, write an essay
/ of at least five paragraphs on one of the topics above. You
must work into your essay *all* the material suggested by
your full thesis. Develop and arrange your paragraphs in
any way that seems effective, bearing in mind that your
purpose is to persuade the reader to agree with your thesis.
NOTE: Hold on to this assignment. You will use it again,
later.

VOCABULARY

1. Find a synonym for each of the following words:

adolescent	flou.ish (*n.*)	modify
analogy	groveling	preamble
belligerent	incoherent	propound
concede	irrelevancy	relevance

2. Use each of the synonyms you have found for the listed
words in a complete sentence. Each sentence must relate
in some way to the problems of essay writing. Be as informal as you please—complain if you feel like it. But use
the synonym, and be sure that your sentence bears some
relation to essay writing. For example, you might write
something like this, using "youthful" (the synonym for one
of the words above):

> It is a cruel and inhuman thing to curb my youthful spirit
> by forcing me to use logic in order to find a thesis.

4

Structure

The basic structure of the essay is extremely simple. It has
three parts: an introduction, a body, and a conclusion—or,
to put it in even simpler terms, a beginning, a middle, and an
end. If this strikes you as painfully obvious, you may be surprised to learn that failure to understand this simple arrangement probably explains the collapse of more essays than any
other single cause.

STRUCTURE

The tendency of the beginning writer is to jump square. into the middle of an essay, unloading information and opinion however it comes to mind. Instead of introducing his subject, he throws it at his reader (and usually misses). Instead of concluding it, he drops the whole thing with a thud or spins it out intolerably because he doesn't know how to stop. All his careful preparation seems to have been for nothing. And the student is unhappily aware of this; he knows that somehow his essay didn't quite come off. He is as disconsolate and uncomprehending as the mad egg-lady who gathers her eggs with exquisite care, packs them delicately into a basket, and then weeps because they break when she dumps them on the floor.

Fortunately, the writer is not in quite so hopeless a position as the egg-lady; if he scrambles his basket of ideas the first time he tries to unload them in writing, he can re-assemble his collection later and begin again. But he can save a great deal of time and wasted effort if he knows in advance what he wants to do with his ideas, if he realizes that when he writes an essay he is confronted not with a dumping process but with a building process.

So think of yourself as a builder. And think of your essay as a *structure*. This basic structure is very simply illustrated in Figure 1.

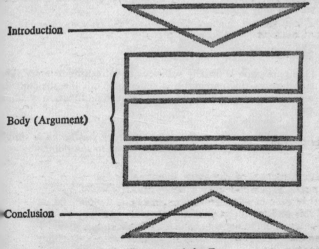

Introduction

Body (Argument)

Conclusion

Figure 1—Structure of the Essay

Think of each of the units in Figure 1 as one paragraph. Certain obvious characteristics show up at once: (1) the first, or introductory, paragraph begins broadly and narrows to a point; (2) the middle section, or "argument," is in block form and takes up most of the space in the essay; and (3) the last, or concluding, paragraph begins at a narrow point and ends broadly.

We will return again and again to this illustration as we progress, demonstrating methods of working with it, of tying the parts firmly together, of enriching it with detail. As it stands now, it represents the "bare bones" of structure, the steel framework upon which every essay must be built. *This basic structure never changes.* It may be so skillfully disguised by the author that you are not aware of its presence, but it is there. You will find it in every successful essay ever written, from the simplest to the most complex. It will differ only in details; the basic structure is always the same.

Just as different architects, beginning with the same basic design, will create completely different houses, so will essayists create different essays. Each will bring his own particular taste and style to his creation; what he is able to do with the basic structure depends upon his imagination, his wit, his vocabulary, his purpose. But he cannot escape the demands of structure.

So let's examine the three main parts of this structure and see how they work.

The Introduction

One paragraph is usually sufficient to introduce an essay. The structure of this paragraph is different from the structure of any other paragraph in the essay because its function is different.

> *The function of the introductory paragraph is simply to introduce the subject and <u>come to the point</u>.*

Figure 2—The Introduction

Examine the sample introduction below:

> The American buggy race is a thing of the past, but its spirit is not. It lives on today at a thousand dragstrips, where teen-age boys now race their hotrods just as their grandfathers once raced their horse-drawn rigs. The boy behind the wheel of that roaring modern buggy, however, has a great deal more than his grandfather's daring spirit. He has a machine built mainly with his own hands and a head full of technical knowledge that grandpa never even dreamed about. Every race he drives is not only a contest but a test—a test of his knowledge as well as his skill as a driver. Like his grandfather, he will race every challenger, but today's drag-racing teen-ager is primarily an automotive engineer, as eager to test his theories as to win races.

The paragraph, you will note, opens with a broad, general statement related to the thesis and then gradually narrows to a single point—the thesis itself. Sentence by sentence it "closes in" on the thesis. Structurally it is a triangle resting on one point (Figure 2). It moves from the general to the specific, from "pan shot" to close-up, from broad observation to punch line.

That is its whole purpose—to introduce the subject in a general way and then come to the point. Here again you can see the psychology of argument in operation. Your thesis, remember, is an *opinion*, and nobody wants an opinion exploding in his face in the first sentence of a conversation, written or oral. (An essay, after all, is a kind of conversation between you and the reader.) So begin your introduction with a general statement and end it with your thesis statement.

Understanding this structure is no problem for most students; the problem is in deciding just what kind of opening statement to make. What can you say that will be not merely a general statement but a general statement that will lead logically into a statement of thesis?

This depends largely upon how you plan to develop your thesis. (Thus you begin to reap immediately the benefits of all that work that went into developing a full thesis statement.) But as a rule of thumb, begin your thinking about an opening statement with one major element in your thesis (usually a noun) and make an observation about it that any sensible reader will find acceptable. In either of the two theses about drag racing, for example, the following two terms are the main elements:

drag racing   teen-agers

Or any of the following could be extracted by inference:

future drivers	responsibility
safety	danger
sport	mechanical skills

In the example on page 43, *race* was used as the key word. But any of the other words extracted from the thesis, directly or by inference, could have served as well:

> Few of the special hobbies of today's youth raise the blood pressure of most adults to the boiling point as quickly as *drag racing*.
> *Teen-agers* seldom cling very long to any of their hobbies.
> In a world already overpopulated with automobiles, the training of *future drivers* becomes a matter of increasing importance.
> *Safety*, unfortunately, is a subject that has little glamour.
> Some kind of *sport* seems to be a natural part of every young man's life.
> Perhaps the most common accusation that adults make against young people today is that they lack a sense of *responsibility*.
> Probably nothing about young people dismays their elders quite so much as their love of *danger*.
> Americans have always excelled in *mechanical skills*.

Any of these opening sentences could lead to either thesis—in favor of drag racing or against it. The author has not yet taken a position. But he has marked out his territory; he has announced generally the subject he is going to cover, and his announcement serves notice that he plans to state a very particular point of view by the end of the paragraph.

A kind of logic asserts itself as you work your way from the opening general statement to the specific thesis. You can see it easily in the example on page 43. The author has chosen to introduce the subject by means of a comparison with the past—one of the simplest of all techniques because we tend to think in terms of time. The sequential logic—from buggy race to hotrod race—is obvious, and it immediately sets up a whole background against which the particular case for or against drag racing can be viewed.

The essay could just as easily have taken off in the opposite direction after the opening statement:

> The American buggy race is a thing of the past, but its spirit is not. Unfortunately, its spirit has undergone almost as complete a transformation as the racetrack and the ve-

hicles themselves. The dirt track of the county fair has become a dragstrip, the buggy has become a hotrod, and the daring but friendly spirit of contest has become a frightening and obsessive competition—often to the death.

It would not be necessary, of course, to start as far back as the buggy with your opening statement:

> The American passion for speed reaches its highest peak of frenzy every year at the Indianapolis Speedway. Such frenzy was bound to spill over into the everyday life of a country addicted to motors. And spill over it has—into thousands of makeshift racetracks where American youngsters put their lives on the line almost daily . . .

From here on, the writer would begin to narrow toward his thesis. Note that it could still go either way. If he adds "in a blind dedication to speed," the thesis will definitely be against drag racing. If he adds "But it is not a blind dedication to speed that motivates the boys on the dragstrips any more than it motivates the skilled mechanics who drive or service the Speedway racers," the thesis will obviously support drag racing.

Other methods of opening with a general statement (without reference to time) can be seen in the samples on page 44. Your choice depends upon the particular emphasis you want to give. But you can be guided by this general rule: your opening statement will *relate* to your thesis but *will not take a position on it.* Then, by a process of qualifying, comparing, illustrating, and gradually limiting the subject, you quietly remove the major obstacles to discussion and get to the point. And there is your thesis at the end of the paragraph, clearly isolated and ready for examination.

No Bombs, Please

One of the commonest errors of beginning writers is to attempt a "terribly clever" opening. You should remember that the demand upon you is for clarity, logic, reasonableness— never for surprise or "gag lines." Your job is to convince the reader of the reasonableness of your thesis and thereby of your reasonableness and wisdom as a human being. *Never* try to be "cute." Almost without exception, the results are disastrous. Consider, for example, these typical "bombshell" openings:

Drag racing! How parents hate it! How kids love it
Zoom! Powie! Varoom! We're off!

or

Whee! Just listen to that roar! The draggers are really
hot tonight.

or

Take four wheels, a little metal and glass and some gaso
line. Mix well and add one boy. What have you got? A
drag racer!

Writing as painfully bad as this is born of a perfectly sound
impulse—the desire to be interesting. Unfortunately, its effec
is exactly the opposite. Almost invariably this kind of "sound
effect" writing is merely a desperate attempt to cover up the
absence of any real thought or imagination. It says nothing
but it makes a great racket. (The exclamation points alone are
almost enough to cause permanent deafness.) The third ex
ample above is less noisy than very, very tired—the old
"recipe-writing dodge" that was never very clever and has no
improved with use. The road to interesting and colorful writ
ing does not lie in this direction.

It lies, first of all, in an understanding of structure. The
lamentable examples above would never have been written if
their student authors had followed the simple structural pat
tern of the introductory paragraph: broad generalization nar
rowing to thesis. Remember, the function of the introductory
paragraph is simply to introduce the subject and come to the
point.

You will discover that it is usually necessary to rewrit
your introduction after you have completed the middle sec
tion of your essay. Often this middle section opens up new
ideas that you will want to incorporate in your introduction
But most writers find they simply cannot get into the main
body of their essays until they have "primed the pump" with
some kind of introduction, even though they must change it
later. So the best policy is to get something down on paper
some general statement leading to your thesis, and then g
back to it later, revising and rewriting as needed.

You may feel at first that the structural pattern of the open
ing paragraph is rigid and limiting, that it does not leave yo
free to be fully creative. It is, indeed, rigid and limiting—
but that is the source of its strength. It provides a steel frame
work upon which you can build confidently. When you have
mastered the basic structure, you can begin to experiment
to take artistic risks with your material. Far from boxing yo

in, the structure sets you free to create, to express fully the best that is in you.

QUESTIONS

1. What is the function of the introductory paragraph?
2. "The introductory paragraph can be described as a triangle resting on one point." Explain.
3. What is the psychological principle behind the practice of opening an introductory paragraph with a broad, noncontroversial statement?
4. What is the rule of thumb for writing the first sentence of an introduction?
5. Explain the meaning of the statement that "the sequential logic—from buggy race to hotrod race—is obvious."
6. Why do students tend to use "bombshell" opening sentences? Why are such sentences nearly always failures?
7. The author suggests that mastery of structure makes it possible for you to express yourself more freely. Explain how this theory might be applied to one of the following activities: dancing, gymnastics, painting, automobile design, dress design.

ASSIGNMENT

1. Write four different opening sentences for the introductory paragraph you wrote for your last essay assignment (pages 39–40), using the structural pattern described in this section.
2. Write the entire introductory paragraph, beginning with one of the opening sentences in #1.
3. Write an introductory paragraph ending with one of the theses below:

    a. Folksinging is more than a fad.
    b. Today's student tends to be a conformist.
    c. The chief purpose of higher education is to teach students to think for themselves.

NOTE: You will need this introductory paragraph for your next two assignments. Hang on to it.

The Big Middle Section

The big middle section of your essay—everything between the introduction and the conclusion—can be almost any length.

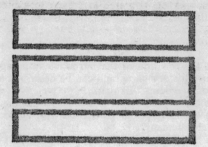

Figure 3—The Middle Section

The number of paragraphs in it depends entirely upon how many points you want to cover and how thoroughly you want to cover them. It would be very foolish to decide in advance precisely how many paragraphs you intend to write— foolish and impossible. All sorts of influences begin working on you when you start writing. You will find yourself thinking, "I'd better use an example here . . . explain a little more clearly there . . . add this point . . . take that one out . . ." Almost the only rule you can follow is this: Write as much as you need to write in order to present your case clearly and completely and persuasively.

> *Whether your middle section is short or long, it is here that the real power of your essay resides. For the middle section is your <u>argument</u>.*

Here you put forward the reasons that will convince the reader of your thesis. And the most brilliant introduction will stagger in mid-flight like a faulty rocket unless you develop the middle section of your essay properly.

Mid-flight power depends upon many things, of course— vocabulary, tone, imagination, originality, style, all the skills of working with language. But the first consideration, the most crucial for the beginner, is *logical development*.

REFER TO YOUR FULL THESIS

Fortunately, you are already perfectly prepared. You took care of that when you worked out your *pro* and *con* arguments for your full thesis statement. There they are, lined up and waiting. Before you have finished writing, you may want to change the order in which you have listed them, but you needn't worry about that yet. Just get started, using your full thesis as a guide. You need only three general rules to guide you:

1st thing

1. *Make the necessary concessions to the opposition as soon as possible.*
2. *Devote at least one paragraph to every major pro argument in your full thesis statement.*
3. *Save your best argument for the last.*

In a short essay you can usually dispose of the opposition with one or two brief sentences. The whole purpose is to concede quickly the points you do not want to dispute, or to set up quickly those that you feel must be disputed, and then get down to business—that is, the presentation of your *pro* arguments only. So you waste no time. Immediately after your introduction, you make any necessary concessions:

Introduction:
> The American buggy race is a thing of the past, but its spirit is not............................
> ....

Thesis: Today's drag-racing teen-ager is primarily an automotive engineer (etc.)

First concession:
> *Admittedly, drag racing has a certain element of danger.* But so has almost every other sport that attracts young men. And drag racing has something that few other sports can claim: an intensely practical value. (Paragraph goes on to develop practical value of drag racing in fostering mechanical skills.)

Second concession:
> *It is true, of course, that drag racing attracts its share of irresponsible idiots.* But. . . . (Paragraph goes on to develop the serious attitude of most racers, their respect for rules, etc.)

Note that these concessions take care of the first two *con* arguments listed on page 37. Each concession opens a paragraph, but the paragraph then moves immediately into a *pro* argument that carries far more weight than the concession. You will probably do this naturally, but it's a good idea to keep the process consciously in mind. Never develop a *con* point as fully as you develop a *pro* point. Obviously if you give more space to your opposition than to your own point of view, you're likely to lose your reader to the enemy camp—or at least make him wonder whether you really believe in your own thesis.

In a short essay two concessions can be joined if they are closely related. The two above, for example, could be placed very easily in one paragraph:

> Admittedly, drag racing has a certain element of danger and attracts its share of irresponsible idiots, but. . . .

Your decision on whether to name certain *con* points jointly or separately depends upon how much emphasis you want to give each point. If you want to give each point a paragraph, name them separately. If they seem so closely related that one paragraph will suffice for both, name them jointly. Never separate them and then repeat the same arguments just to fill up space. That never fools readers (or teachers). It simply bores and exasperates them beyond endurance.

In a very short essay, you may be able to dismiss all the opposition with a single concession. But if your thesis requires considerable explanation or a very involved defense, you may find it necessary to devote a full paragraph to explaining an opposition point. In that case you must follow it immediately with a full paragraph—or more—in defense of your own position. It's a simple matter of self-preservation. Never allow an opposing point of view to appear stronger than your own.

Whatever the length of the essay, the main idea is to get the opposition out of the way as soon as possible, both in the essay itself and in the individual paragraphs. For a clearer understanding of this structure, study Figures 4 and 5, on pages 51–52.

Note that the final paragraphs are devoted exclusively to *pro* arguments. It is always a mistake to allow reservations or concessions to crop up late; it weakens the essay disastrously. Your final paragraphs must be strong and assured, ringing with authority and conviction. Having vanquished your enemy, you need no longer concern yourself with him. You have the floor, and you proceed confidently to take full advantage of it.

YOUR STRONGEST ARGUMENT

Remember that your final argument in this middle section should be your strongest. Naturally the question arises, "How do I tell which argument is strongest?"

The argument that *seems* strongest to you, the one that may have finally decided you in favor of your particular

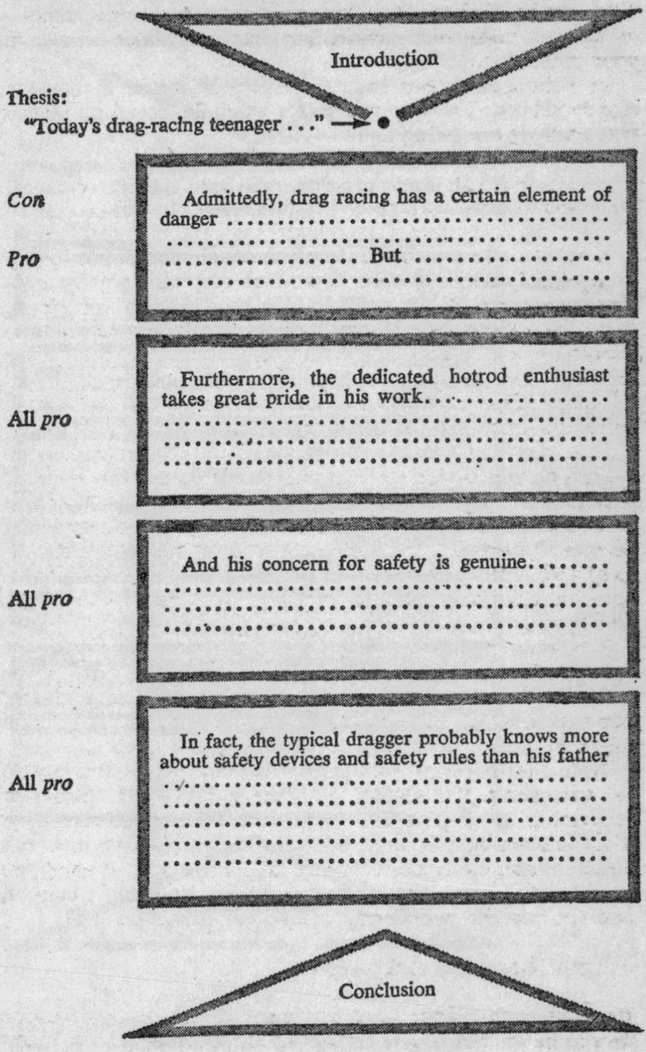

Introduction

Thesis:

"Today's drag-racing teenager . . ." →•

Con

Admittedly, drag racing has a certain element of danger . . . .

Pro

. . . . But . . . .

All pro

Furthermore, the dedicated hotrod enthusiast takes great pride in his work. . . . .

All pro

And his concern for safety is genuine. . . . .

All pro

In fact, the typical dragger probably knows more about safety devices and safety rules than his father . . . .

Conclusion

Figure 4—The Short Essay

you can put all cons tog (1st #)

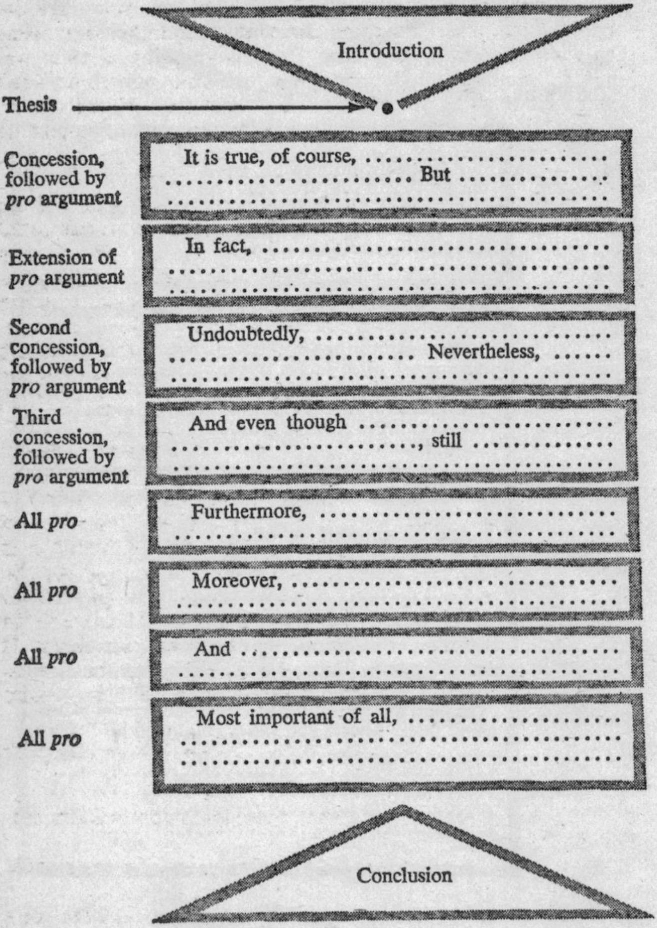

Introduction

Thesis ⟶ •

Concession, followed by *pro* argument	It is true, of course, ... But ....
Extension of *pro* argument	In fact, ...
Second concession, followed by *pro* argument	Undoubtedly, ... Nevertheless, ...
Third concession, followed by *pro* argument	And even though ...., still ....
All *pro*	Furthermore, ...
All *pro*	Moreover, ...
All *pro*	And ....
All *pro*	Most important of all, ...

Conclusion

Figure 5—The Longer Essay *

---

* Bear in mind that the arrangement of early paragraphs here is suggested only. You may want to devote an entire paragraph to a concession or add extra "extensions" of *pro* arguments. But later paragraphs should concentrate on *pro* arguments only, as shown.

thesis, will probably be the strongest for your essay. But this is not always true—particularly if your emotions are involved. Remember that argument with your father over using the car? The strongest reason from your point of view was the date you had already made. But such an argument wouldn't cut much ice with your father—not after that dented fender. So you must be sure, in selecting your strongest argument, to base your choice not merely upon personal feeling but upon a sensible awareness of your reader's point of view.

Sometimes in the very process of writing you will find the relative strength of an argument changing. A reason that seemed minor when you first wrote your full thesis may suddenly acquire new meaning and importance through a good example, a new insight, an unexpected phrase. In some mysterious way your writing becomes more vivid and interesting. Looking over your essay later you will think, "That's the best point of all!" In that case it should be moved to the last position, and all other arguments should be used as steppingstones to this major paragraph.

In short, *the middle section of your essay should always move toward its most telling paragraph.* Never commit yourself in advance to a rigid ordering of paragraphs. Your full thesis is a guide, remember, not a straitjacket. If your essay is humorous, that last paragraph should be the funniest; if your essay emphasizes logic, the last paragraph should be the ultimate in logic; if your essay attempts to present an extremely complex idea, your paragraphs should move from the simplest possible presentation to whatever complexity is required to make your point. This is your last chance to convince your reader. Give him the best you have; this is where you clinch the argument. *from reader's p. of v.*

QUESTIONS

1. "The real power of your essay resides in the middle section." Explain.
2. How does the full thesis help you in preparing the middle section?
3. Describe the method of handling opposition in both long and short essays.
4. What point should you make last in your argument? Why?

ASSIGNMENT

4. Write a middle section to follow the introduction you wrote for Assignment 3 (page 47). Use the illustration for either

the short or the long essay (Figures 4 and 5) as a guide.
NOTE: Hold on to this assignment. You will need it later.

The Conclusion

You have introduced your subject, presented your thesis, and defended it. One step remains. You must wrap things up in one last paragraph and gracefully withdraw: you must write a conclusion. Otherwise, no matter how thoroughly you have explored every point in your full thesis, your essay will remain a piece of unfinished business, as unsatisfying as a piece of music that never hits its final note.

A student writer who has made his way through most of his essay with style and dash often finds himself baffled by the attempt to conclude. He is like the guest who doesn't quite know how to go home, standing irresolutely at the door, unable to bring himself to open it, forcing the conversation to go on and on—and driving his hosts mad (or putting them, finally, to sleep). Eventually, incapable of leaving gracefully, he makes a wild bolt for it—which means, in the essayist's terms, that he doesn't write a conclusion at all.

"But I haven't anything else to say," the student complains. "I've used up everything in my full thesis. Where do I look now for ideas?"

The answer may come as a surprise. Look in your introduction.

BACK TO BEGINNINGS

You have come a long way from that opening paragraph. How can you make a connection at this late date with those distant sentences, written when your essay was only a few notes on a card?

You not only *can* make a connection, you *must* make it if the paragraphs you have written so far are ever to take on the solid shape and feel of an essay.

Since so much depends upon this connection, it makes sense to take a final, critical look at your introduction. Can you see any way to improve that first paragraph? In all likelihood, you can. The process of writing the middle section nearly always opens your eyes to new possibilities for your introduction. So double back. Now is the time to rewrite it if it needs rewriting. Any improvements you can make will almost certainly be reflected in your conclusion.

Then, with your introduction in its best possible shape, it is time to think about your conclusion.

UNDERSTAND THE STRUCTURE

Again, an understanding of basic structure can help you. The structure of the conclusion (Figure 6) is exactly the reverse of the structure underlying your introduction, which began with a broad general statement and narrowed to its point, or thesis.

Figure 6—The Conclusion

> *Your conclusion begins with the thesis and widens gradually toward a final broad statement.*

So, to get your conclusion started, simply repeat your thesis sentence, adding an appropriate word or phrase, if necessary, to tie it in properly with the paragraph that preceded it:

> Thesis: Today's drag-racing teen-ager is primarily an automotive engineer. . . .
>
> Restated thesis: In short, today's drag-racing teen-ager is, primarily, an automotive engineer. . . .

And the first sentence of your conclusion is already written for you. You need only lift it out of your introduction and drop it into place.

Often, however, this straight transfer of thesis seems flat and uninteresting. In that case, vary the wording. You can vary it in dozens of ways without changing the meaning. The following variations, for example, do the trick without repeating the exact words of the thesis:

> Clearly then, this young man is no irresponsible bum; he's an automotive engineer. . . .
>
> An automotive engineer, an expert driver, a specialist in safety—that is the real definition of today's drag racer. . . .

From this point you will begin to broaden toward your final sentence. As you do so, you can make a still stronger connection with your introduction by picking up any significant word or phrase in it and working it into your conclusion. Every time you do this you create echoes in a reader's mind, touch a nerve of remembrance. You might, for example, use the word "buggy" in your next sentence—"He may contrast strangely with his buggy-driving ancestors . . ."—thus sounding a note you struck in your opening sentence (see sample introduction, page 43).

When you create an echo like this, the reader does not say to himself consciously, "Oh, yes, that was mentioned earlier." He simply has that particular sense of satisfaction and completion that comes to all of us when we feel that everything is falling into place, that things "fit."

Sometimes it is possible to conclude a very short essay by borrowing only from the introduction. Ordinarily, however, you need further ties with the middle section in order to give your conclusion substance.

TYING IN THE MIDDLE SECTION

Many student essays run aground in the final paragraph because the writer attempts to summarize the points he has made simply by listing them. "In the preceding paragraphs it was shown that drag racers are good mechanics, that they are expert drivers, and that they are safe drivers." This listing of points, as though you are adding up a column of figures, is deadly. Your reader does not like to be reminded in this heavy-handed way of something he has just finished reading.

Try, instead, to suggest, to leave your reader with a series of pictures in his mind rather than a series of blunt and graceless declarations. Borrow meaning from your middle section, borrow a few key words, but don't be flatly repetitive, don't make lists. Say what you have already said, but say it sharply, quickly, and in different words. Look at the difference in the two sample conclusions below, both written for an essay that stressed the drag racer's mechanical skill, his pride in workmanship, and his knowledge of safety:

> Therefore, today's drag-racing teen-ager is primarily an automotive engineer. The preceding paragraphs have shown that he has a great deal of mechanical skill, he takes pride in his workmanship, and he has much knowledge of safety.

> Clearly, then, the typical drag-racing teen-ager is no irresponsible bum, but a genuine automotive engineer. His mechanical skill verges on inventive genius, and his pride in workmanship is a sign of his maturity. Furthermore, he could give most adults lessons in safety.

The first example repeats the thesis verbatim and summarizes the points as if they were items on a laundry list. The second varies the words of the thesis and disperses the points in two separate (and differently constructed) sentences. With one or two more sentences, the paragraph could move outward, relating drag racing to a broader background and closing on a final, authoritative note:

> . . . One thing is certain: the drag racer is a product of his times. The society he lives in has been shaped by the automobile, and drag racing is as natural to him as buggy racing was to his grandfather. Society might as well learn not only to accept him but to appreciate his talents. He'll be around as long as we keep moving on wheels. And that is likely to be a very long time indeed.

And the essay has reached its end. The conclusion, borrowing from everything that has gone before, summarizing without repeating exactly, has given the essay its final shape, has made it into a whole, compact, self-sustaining unit.

Borrow. Suggest. Transform. Pull out words and phrases and place them in a new setting. *Remind your reader.* Then move outward with a statement that relates your thesis to a broader background, so that he can see it in a last long perspective.

Remember, your conclusion is your last word with your reader, your last chance to persuade him of the truth in your thesis. Take advantage of it.

Summary

Think of your essay as a structure, as something that you actually build according to a definite architectural pattern. You will find it far easier to say what you want to say when you have a sense of structure, for it imposes on your thoughts the discipline of logic, which in turn develops your ability to organize and to make relationships.

Every essay has three major parts: an introduction that states the thesis and that can be seen structurally as a triangle resting on one point; a middle section, structurally a large block, made up of several smaller blocks of argument; and a conclusion, another triangle resting on a broad-based generalization related to the rest of the essay. Whether an essay is long or short it will have this structure, and you can learn specific techniques for writing each of the three major structural parts and relating them to one another.

Once you have mastered this structure you are ready for the really exciting part of writing: the study of style. That begins in the next chapter. Most of the writing you have done so far has simply familiarized you with your instrument. Soon you will discover what kind of music it can make. But be sure you know your instrument first. Stay with structure until you understand it thoroughly.

QUESTIONS

1. Since the middle section of an essay covers all the points in the full thesis, why does an essay need a concluding paragraph?
2. How does the introduction help you write a conclusion?
3. Why is it likely that you will need to rewrite your introduction before writing a conclusion?
4. Describe the structure of a conclusion.
5. "Every time you pick up a significant word or phrase from preceding paragraphs and work it into your conclusion you create echoes in a reader's mind." Explain this statement.
6. How can you summarize without listing?
7. Explain what is meant by "broadening" your concluding paragraph to its final sentence.

ASSIGNMENT

5. Look again at the introduction and middle section that you wrote for Assignments 3 and 4. Rewrite your introduction. Then write a concluding paragraph.
6. Write a complete essay on one of the following subjects:

cats	basketball	careers
dogs	football	college
horses	track	money problems

VOCABULARY

1. Using your dictionary, write a definition for each of the following words:

argument	lamentable	tendency
disconsolate	obsessive	close-up
intolerably	repetitive	pan shot
irresolutely	sequential	

2. Each of the words above is used here in a complete sentence followed by part of another sentence. Finish each of the incomplete sentences so that it *explains or illustrates* the first sentence.

 a. Most people think of an argument as a quarrel. In an essay, however, an argument . . .
 b. She was disconsolate. She . . .
 c. The man was intolerably rude. He . . .
 d. The boy stood irresolutely at the door. He could not decide whether to . . .
 e. Her wardrobe was in lamentable condition. Everything she owned . . .
 f. The man showed obsessive concern for his health in many ways. He . . .
 g. He made some good points, but he was repetitive. I got tired of . . .
 h. The problems were arranged in sequential order, according to their difficulty. The most difficult problem . . .
 i. She has a tendency to be overcritical. She seems to feel that . . .
 j. The close-up scenes were particularly effective. One shot concentrated on the old man's hands, and you could see . . .
 k. Films often open with a wide pan shot. In a western movie, for example, the camera usually sets the scene by . . .

5

First Steps Toward Style

By now you should have the "feel" of an essay, the sense of it as a structure. Structure alone, however, does not guarantee a good essay any more certainly than an artist's first charcoal sketch on canvas guarantees a good oil painting. The original sketch may be strong, interesting, and full of promise, but the final judgment of the work rests upon the artist's use of his paints.

In the same way, the final judgment of a piece of writing depends upon the writer's use of words.

You may have a brilliant thesis. You may have devised

for it an impressive structure, unassailable in its logic and perfect in its proportions. And you will have thus proved that you can think and that you can organize—two skills essential to good writing. But now you are face to face with the actual job of *writing,* of choosing the words and shaping the sentences and developing the paragraphs that will say best, most clearly and effectively, exactly what you want to say.

You are, in short, up against the problem of *style.*

Style in writing is like style in anything else—some special quality that commands interest or gives pleasure, something that makes you "sit up and take notice." It shows up in all sorts of places, and it's always easy to spot. At a basketball game, for example, you may find yourself watching one particular player most of the time. He may not be the team's highest scorer, but it's such a pleasure to watch him in action that he stands out from all the others. Pressed to explain why his performance gives you pleasure, you might say, "He seems to do everything so easily."

That's style.

Style is perhaps best defined as this ability to do something difficult as though it were easy. Invariably we respond to it with delight. We may appreciate the points made for our team by the ballplayer who pants and stumbles and strains for every shot, but the player who gets our praise is the one whose every move seems effortless.

The principle is the same in writing. You are bored by the writer who makes his point laboriously, painfully, in dull and awkward language. Yet a writer who makes exactly the same point without apparent effort, in language that seems as easy to understand as good conversation, will hold your interest.

This air of effortlessness, whether in ball playing or writing (or, for that matter, in singing or dancing or playing ping-pong or juggling six ripe oranges), is deceptive. For its secret is control. And control is a hard-won thing. Your ballplayer didn't have that perfect hook-shot handed to him on a platter by Mother Nature. He *learned* it—and he learned it through hours of patient, disciplined practice in an empty gym. No writer is born knowing how to put words together to best effect. He *learns* this skill, and he learns it in the same way the ballplayer learns his—through self-discipline and practice.

Style, in other words, is not a mysterious gift reserved for the lucky few. It is something you learn. You may feel that you have no talent for writing, no special gift. And you may be entirely correct in this assessment of your abilities. "Nobody," you may say, "can learn to be talented." Correct again. But you *can* learn style. For style is not a gift. It is technique.

It is the "how" of writing as opposed to the "what." No matter what you have to say, you can learn to say it well. And that is style.

It takes practice. You must perfect your ability to handle language through hard work with paper and pencil. This means learning not only what to do but what *not* to do.

And that is the place to begin.

You are about to be presented with two rules that may strike you as peculiar or simply maddening or downright irrelevant. Peculiar they certainly are, for you will learn them for only one reason: so that you can break them intelligently when you are more experienced. And maddening they may well be, for they may cut you off from the only kind of writing that makes you feel secure. But irrelevant they are not. They will teach you quickly some things about style in writing that would take years to learn through trial and error.

Bear in mind that these rules are temporary. When you have practiced them long enough to make them part of your working equipment, you can break them with the assurance that you know exactly what you are doing. But for the present, until and unless you are otherwise instructed, they are to be your Two Commandments:

1. *Do not use first person.*
2. *Do not use the word "there"—ever.*

The First Commandment

In most of the essays or themes that you have written in the past, you have probably made liberal use of the personal pronoun. Youthful efforts at self-expression are nearly always thick with "I think . . . ," "I believe . . . ," "I feel that . . . ," "It is my opinion. . . ." The habit of using the personal pronoun to express an opinion is, in fact, so ingrained in some students that they honestly believe it is impossible to express an opinion without using the word "I."

They are mistaken. The truth is that an opinion is almost always more forceful and convincing if it is presented without the personal pronoun. In the following pairs, which statement carries more conviction?

A. I believe that God exists.
B. God exists.

A. It is my opinion that smoking causes cancer.
B. Smoking causes cancer.

A. I think drag racing trains automotive engineers.
B. Drag racing trains automotive engineers.

Obviously the second statement of each pair carries far more punch than the first—*and it says exactly the same thing.* It merely says it more briefly, more forcefully, with a greater air of authority. Whenever a phrase containing a personal pronoun is attached to an opinion, the opinion immediately becomes weak and defensive. It sounds vaguely apologetic. That nervous "I think . . ." seems to imply, "What I think isn't very important, but anyway I think that . . ."

The fact is, of course, that the student who feels compelled to attach a personal pronoun to all his thoughts is not really writing about his subject at all. He is writing about himself. He is pushing himself between the reader and the subject— usually to the reader's great annoyance. Notice, in the examples following, how surgery on the personal pronouns forces the real subject to the fore:

> I think a good way to handle this matter is by student-body vote. I don't see how anybody could object to that.
>
> A good way to handle this matter is by student-body vote. Nobody could object to that.
>
> To me, Mark Twain's writing is very funny, but I think it is also very bitter.
>
> Mark Twain's writing is very funny and very bitter.
>
> I never know what to think when people behave like that.
>
> Such behavior is always puzzling.

It is helpful to remember that "I think" and "I feel" and similar expressions are actually redundant—they aren't needed, and they get in the reader's way. As the writer, you are always lurking in the background of your essay. Your reader knows this. He knows that every opinion you express is yours unless you state otherwise, so why add an "I think" to it? Obviously you think it or you wouldn't say it.

But don't try to conceal an "I think" or a "My opinion is" by converting it to a phrase like "The writer thinks" or "In the opinion of the writer." This is merely substitute first person; it replaces the personal pronoun with an even more annoying obstacle to the reader's wish to get at the meaning of a sentence. The personal pronoun, instead of disappearing entirely, merely hides itself under a layer of cotton wool. Sentences like this develop:

In the opinion of the writer, something should be done about the problem immediately.

This writer believes that girls spend too much time on their hair.

Notice how much crisper, how much more direct and authoritative the sentences become, after surgery:

Something should be done about the problem immediately.
Girls spend too much time on their hair.

The urge to use first person is so powerful that few students can give it up without a struggle. Many try to take refuge in the impersonal *one* ("One never knows what might happen") or the second-person *you* ("You can't help liking this book") or, as a last sad resort, a substitute second person ("A person should always have a good study plan"). Surgery will not work for these. If you cut them out entirely, the rest of the sentence won't make sense. So the thought must be rephrased, using third person:

Not: One never knows what might happen.	(Impersonal)
But: Anything might happen.	(Third person)
Not: You can't help liking this book.	(Second person)
But: This book is irresistible.	(Third person)
Not: A person should always have a good study plan.	(Substitute second person)
But: A good study plan is essential.	(Third person)

Notice that in each case the sentence becomes not only more direct and vigorous—it becomes *shorter*. Yet its meaning remains exactly the same. You have simply cut out all the words that contribute nothing to meaning or style. And that is one reason for restricting yourself, for the present, to writing in third person. It offers valuable training in the art of saying what you mean, directly and forcefully.

This is not to say that you should never use first or second person. Some of the finest essays in the language have been written in first person. And this textbook makes liberal use of second person because it tends to personalize instructional materials. But you must earn your right to use these other modes of address. And you earn it by learning first of all to speak with authority and assurance in third person.

So train yourself to write, for the time being, in third person only. It is a habit that offers many unexpected rewards. You will find yourself thinking clearly rather than feeling vaguely. You will concentrate on your subject with greater intensity, thus discovering not only more things to say but more direct and vigorous ways of saying them. Above all, you will be more logical—and, for the essayist, logic is the basic weapon. Third person forces you to be logical, for it requires you to throw away the crutch of the personal pronoun and to consider your arguments with the same kind of coolness and detachment that you can expect from your reader.

Mastery of third person will give you a powerful new sense of authority and control. Gradually this new sense will make itself felt in everything you write. When you finally return to first person (as you will, in later assignments), you will be able to use it far more effectively than ever before.

The full command of third person is not something you are likely to achieve overnight. Your first attempts at it, in fact, may be accompanied by howls of frustration. But with practice you will discover its enormous range and flexibility, its potential not only for brisk and forceful statement but for graceful expression.

So practice it. In the assignment at the end of this chapter, and in all the assignments for the next several chapters, you will be limited strictly to third person. You have been using first and second person, and awkward substitutes for first and second person, as crutches. Now you must put your crutches aside and learn to walk alone.

Don't worry if you stumble a bit at first. Eventually you'll find your balance.

The Second Commandment

Don't use the word "there."

An easy rule to follow? Don't be too sure. If you are like most people, you probably haven't the faintest notion of how often you use this harmless-looking little five-letter word. Stopping its use may be almost as hard as stopping a nervous habit like doodling or eraser-nibbling. You don't even know you're doing it until somebody points it out to you.

The trouble with "there" has nothing to do with grammar or with "correctness" of any kind. It's a perfectly proper word, and it moves in the best circles; you will find it in abundance in the work of the most distinguished writers. But the fact remains that it is one of the most insidious enemies a beginning writer faces in his search for style.

It is the enemy of style because it seldom adds anything but clutter to a sentence. And nothing saps the vitality of language as quickly as meaningless clutter. Look at this sentence:

There was something wrong.

Now look at the same sentence without the "there."

Something was wrong.

The greater urgency of the second sentence should be obvious; of the two, it's the one more likely to convince you that something is *really* wrong. As a reader you are alerted by that direct, straight-to-the-heart-of-the-matter statement. Clutter it up with "there was" and all the strength oozes out of the sentence.

Sometimes you need only cross out "there" and juggle the words slightly to create a better, more direct sentence. But this won't always work. What would you do, for example, with a sentence like this?

There was a fight.

If you cross out the word "there," you won't have the right words to make a sentence. Even after juggling, the best you can come up with is this:

A fight was.

And that doesn't make sense. (To see how silly it can look, try it in context with one or two other sentences: "The crowd grew bigger. A fight was. The police had to be called.")

Obviously, the trouble is not merely with "there" but with the two words, "there was." Remove both of them, and you are left with the one important element in the sentence—a fight. Ask yourself what verb would work with it, and your problem is solved:

A fight *broke out.*
A fight *developed.*
A fight *erupted.*

Any one of these or several others (*began, started, ensued, threatened*) would do the job—although *erupted* is probably best because it is the most graphic. The point is that any appropriate active verb will give your sentence more life and vigor than the flabby and colorless "there was" construction.

Frequently a sentence containing this construction will end in a prepositional phrase:

Somewhere there was the creaking sound of a door.

Again, by taking out the "there was" you are left with something that is not a sentence. But you can make it into a sentence with remarkable ease by moving the object of the preposition so that it becomes the subject:

Somewhere a door . . .

Add a verb and you will have a sentence that says in four words what it took nine words to say when you used "there was":

Somewhere a door *creaked*.

You could have written, of course, "Somewhere a door made a creaking sound." But that is a waste of words—you are using four words (*made a creaking sound*) to say what could be said more crisply with one (*creaked*). One characteristic of a good style is the ability to pack as much meaning as possible, without loss of clarity, into as few words as possible.

Then there was a speech by Henry.
Then Henry spoke.
Suddenly there was the sound of a motor.
Suddenly a motor roared into life.
At midnight there was a break in the dam.
At midnight the dam burst.

Rip out "there was" and immediately Henry's speech is a little more important, the sound of the motor a little louder, the breaking of the dam somehow more disastrous. Why? Because each statement has become sharper, more direct, through the removal of meaningless words and the addition of active verbs: *spoke, roared, burst*.

Never underestimate the power of an active verb. And never underestimate the weakness of a pure verb (*is, was, are, were, have been, had been*, etc.), particularly when it is attached to the word "there." Pure verbs are simply verbs of *being;* they indicate existence and nothing else—no motion, no color, no sound. They turn sentences into mere snapshots of arrested movement, mere echoes of sound: "There was thunder and lightning." Active verbs are verbs of *doing;* they turn sentences into motion pictures with sound and color: "Thunder crashed" (or *roared* or *grumbled* or *muttered*); "Lightning flashed across the sky" (or *streaked* or *sliced* or *split* or *stitched* or *zigzagged*).

Our language is rich with active verbs; they are available by the thousand, ready to carry any shade of meaning. Yet the sad truth is that we make far too little use of them. With all these riches in the bank we continue to write like paupers. And the "there-plus-pure-verb" habit is largely responsible. Only after you have conquered the habit will you begin to draw on the wealth of active verbs that can give your writing life and strength.

Sometimes, of course, a "there" is really needed, as in the sentence, "I was there" (meaning literally, "I was in that place"). The word "there," used in this strict sense, is probably the clearest and simplest way to express your meaning.

Nevertheless, for the time being you must avoid even this use. It's too easy to confuse a necessary "there" with a merely convenient "there." So avoid the word entirely. Kick it out of your vocabulary. Banish it. Send it to Siberia. As far as you are concerned, the word "there" is poison, and *you are not to use it at all*.

That won't be easy. "There" is such a small word, so modest and well-behaved and familiar, that you literally no longer see it. You must learn to scan your written work with a cold, objective eye for every hidden "there," to yank it out along with its lackluster verb, and to shape new sentences from the remains of the old.

This shaping of new sentences will lead you to new discoveries about language—its richness, its flexibility, its possibilities. You will learn what it means to *play* with language—to experiment, to juggle words into new patterns, to pick up sentences by their tails and turn them around, to pick and choose from a new wealth of verbs.

And when you have learned to do this you will have come a long way toward style.

Summary

The "two commandments" represent way stations on the road to style. You have not yet finished with structure, but from this point forward structure and style begin to merge. So you need to arm yourself now with the two commandments; they can give you immeasurable help in the writing that lies ahead. *Get rid of "there." Get rid of first person.* Learn to do without them now in your writing, and when they are returned to you—as they will be—you will be able to handle them with grace and skill.

The exercises that follow will help you establish the habit of writing in third person without the help of "there." Then you will be ready to practice your new discipline in the paragraph, which comes next.

QUESTIONS

1. In what way is style in writing similar to style in any kind of activity?
2. Why is it important to learn what *not* to do in writing? Give an example of the value of this rule in some other field (golfing, bowling, swimming, acting, singing, etc.).
3. Name the two rules that you are to observe in your writing until further notice.
4. Why does the use of the personal pronoun frequently weaken a writer's statement? To support your answer, give examples other than those used in the text.
5. What is meant by the terms "substitute first person" and "substitute second person"?
6. How does the elimination of the word "there" from your written work force you to use better verbs?

ASSIGNMENT

1. Complete the sentences below so that they express your personal opinion:

   a. I think that student clubs . . .
   b. In my opinion, art classes . . .
   c. To me, the best movies . . .
   d. I feel that a college education . . .
   e. It is my belief that the color of a man's skin . . .
   f. One must pay close attention to most scientific lectures if . . .
   g. If you analyze television programming, you discover that . . .
   h. I don't see the point in requiring a person to . . .
   i. I feel almost certain that space travel . . .
   j. Nobody can convince me that . . .

2. Rewrite each one of your sentences in strict third person, avoiding all use of *I, me, my, one, you, a person,* etc.
3. Delete the word "there" from all the sentences below. Rewrite the sentences if necessary, using active verbs whenever possible.

   a. There is a girl in math class who has a brain like a computer.
   b. There are some aspects of this problem which can never be understood.
   c. Every member of the team was there when the coach made the announcement.
   d. There will be plenty to eat.
   e. If there is one thing he can't stand, it's long telephone conversations.
   f. He was right, but there were moments when she hated him for it.
   g. There will be no meeting of the club tomorrow.
   h. There were lots of good things to eat in the basket.
   i. There was a crowd of happy students in the hall.
   j. His point of view is strange, but there is a lot to be said in its favor.

VOCABULARY

1. Look up the definition of the following adjectives:

   authoritative   objective
   insidious   redundant

2. In one sentence for each, explain exactly what the writer means in the sentences below. (Do not repeat the italicized word nor any form of it.)

   a. He could speak with an *authoritative* voice on the subject of space flight.
   b. His political enemies tried to destroy him by *insidious* attacks on his loyalty.
   c. She seemed utterly incapable of an *objective* point of view.
   d. Don't make *redundant* comments.

6

The Size and Shape
of Middle Paragraphs

Just as the structure of an introduction or a conclusion can be represented as a triangle, the structure of middle paragraphs can be represented graphically as rectangles, or "blocks" (Figure 7). It is helpful to think of these paragraphs quite literally as blocks—blocks of writing firmly divided from each other and making up the body of your essay.

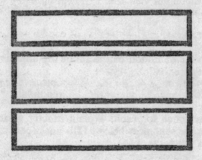

Figure 7—The Size and Shape of Middle Paragraphs

You have been writing middle paragraphs all along, of course, with each essay assignment you have completed. But chances are you have never been entirely certain that your paragraphs succeeded—nor indeed that they were really paragraphs. What goes into a paragraph? How long should it be? How do you know where to start and when to stop? Exactly what *is* a paragraph? These are the questions that plague most students.

Occasionally you may be tempted to begin a new paragraph simply because you have the uneasy feeling that a particular block of writing is too long; you think the page will *look* better if you indent. So, willy-nilly, you indent, trusting to luck that the new arrangement is a paragraph.

Actually, such a principle is not all bad. The page *will* look better. An enormous, uninterrupted block of writing is a formidable thing on a page. It looks difficult and dull (and it usually is). The eye longs for variety, for pause, for some relief in the monotony of an unchanging typographical landscape. And that is one of the reasons for paragraphing: it makes the purely physical job of reading a great deal easier.

But that is only one of the reasons for paragraphing, and a minor one at that. If paragraphing involved no more than this, you could slice up long stretches of writing with a pair of scissors and call each slice a paragraph. Undoubtedly the new arrangement would look more interesting. Unfortunately, however, it wouldn't make much sense. (If you don't believe this, try typing out an essay from your literature text without paragraphing it. Then slice it into uniform pieces, paste it back together with each piece representing a paragraph, and read it. It will give you quite a jolt.) Obviously, something a great deal more important than mere eye-appeal is involved in paragraphing.

The important thing involved is, of course, ideas. The whole purpose of paragraphing is to separate ideas, to give each one its own setting so that it can be fully and clearly developed without interference from others.

Your first guide to this division-by-idea is your full thesis statement.

One Point, One Paragraph

Each of the major points you want to make in your essay is listed in your full thesis statement. Thus, if you have listed three points, you are automatically committed to at least three middle paragraphs.

But that's a bare minimum, hardly more than a starting point. For if your essay has any substance at all, each of your major points is likely to need considerably more discussion than a single paragraph can handle. In fact, it is very nearly impossible to state a major argument completely in one paragraph, simply because it *is* a major argument. It's so important that you will find yourself adding an example here, clearing up a question there, commenting on related side issues. Thus one major point may multiply into several paragraphs, each with its own small point to make.

Perhaps the easiest way to decide whether a minor point

deserves a paragraph of its own is to think of your writing as talk. Each time that you would say, in conversation, "Oh, and by the way . . ." or "Listen, here's another thing . . ." you would, in writing, start a new paragraph.

That's really just about all that paragraphing amounts to.

Length of Paragraphs

It is impossible to predetermine the exact length of any paragraph, just as it is impossible to predetermine the length of any essay. Too much depends upon what you want to say and how you want to say it.

You have often seen paragraphs that are very brief indeed —mere flashes of thought thrust between heavier blocks of writing. Sometimes a single sentence, even a single phrase, will have full paragraph indentation.

Like this.

Such fragments, however, are not really paragraphs. They are rhetorical devices, attention-getters. They can be very effective, but their effectiveness depends mainly upon their contrast with the fully developed paragraphs around them.

You must therefore learn first the "feel" of a real paragraph, acquire a sense of what to put in, what to leave out, and where to stop. You can do this best by thinking in terms of big, fully developed paragraphs.

Try for a paragraph six or seven sentences long, with a total of 100 to 125 words. That's a fairly substantial paragraph. By setting the length at this point you force yourself to "think long," to exercise your imagination and ingenuity. Most students complain of being unable to find enough to fill out a paragraph; they express their main idea in one sentence and then sit paralyzed, unable to think of anything else to say. But an understanding of paragraph structure will soon cure this problem. In fact, you are likely to find it hard to keep paragraphs short enough after you understand their structure. But it is far easier to shrink a paragraph after it is written than to expand it. So try for the big paragraph.

Basic Paragraph Structure

The block structure of middle paragraphs (Figure 7), as opposed to the triangular structure of introductory and concluding paragraphs (Figures 2 and 6), should suggest immediately their major characteristic: they are solid, self-contained, fully developed units. Instead of moving toward or away from a point, each one *is* a point—a single point enlarged into a block of argument.

These blocks are, of course, related to each other, since each of them has the same basic purpose—to explain or illustrate some part of your thesis. Furthermore, they are linked together in various ways that you will study later. But in a very real sense, every paragraph is complete in itself. It can stand alone, with its own particular feeling of wholeness.

If you examine the block structure of a paragraph closely, you will discover that something rather interesting is going on inside it: the structural pattern of the essay is repeating itself.

> *Like the essay itself, every paragraph has three parts:*
> *a beginning, a middle, and an end.*

That's why it has a feeling of completeness. In effect, every paragraph is a miniature essay.

Nothing clears up the mystery of paragraphing so quickly as this realization that a paragraph has three parts, a structure of its own. It has a *beginning*, called the topic sentence. It has a *middle*, consisting of several sentences that explain and illustrate the topic sentence. And it has an *ending*, called the concluding sentence.

The topic sentence, always the first sentence of the paragraph, is simply an announcement of the particular point to be taken up in the paragraph. The point, of course, will be one of those you have listed in your full thesis statement, or a related sub-point. Simply write a complete sentence that sets this point forth clearly. That's your topic sentence. It tells your reader what the paragraph is *about*.

Follow this topic sentence with several sentences that explain and illustrate your point. That's your paragraph's middle-section. And the very act of filling this out will drive you naturally toward a concluding sentence, a final flourish of words that seem to say "and that takes care of *that*."

As soon as you begin to follow this three-part paragraph structure, you will discover that the "one point, one paragraph" rule will take care of itself. For if you introduce your paragraph with a topic sentence, devote the middle of the paragraph to explaining and illustrating the topic sentence, and then draw your conclusion, you can't miss. You will have, automatically, a one-point paragraph.

The topic sentence and concluding sentence offer few problems. It's those middle sentences that dismay most students:

What comes between the topic sentence and the concluding sentence? How can you stick to the point without repeating yourself? How, in other words, do you develop a paragraph?

The answer is surprisingly simple.

Developing a Paragraph

Once you have stated your topic sentence, you do the most natural thing in the world: you explain and illustrate it.

You do this every day, unconsciously, in your conversation:

> "Man, I've never seen such a traffic jam. Cars were lined up all the way to Maxwell Bridge. Everybody was honking, and some guy in a blue Buick back of me was yelling like a madman—said he'd miss his plane and he'd sue the mayor or something. . . ."

> "It was hard work. Up every morning at five and out in the fields by six. Digging holes for fenceposts, running the tractor, hoeing corn—you should have seen the blisters on my hands the first week. . . ."

> "I'm scared to death of dentists. The minute I sit down in that chair, my knees turn to water and the old pulse goes up to about 180. . . ."

These are just random bits of talk, the kind you use or overhear every day. The speaker might wind up his part in the conversation with something like this:

> "Man, I've never seen such a traffic jam. . . . . It was probably the biggest snafu in the history of the automobile."

> "It was hard work. . . . . I never worked so hard in my whole life."

> "I'm scared to death of dentists. . . . . One look at a dentist, and I turn into the world's biggest coward."

Observe the pattern. First the speaker makes it clear that he is talking about something in particular: a traffic jam, hard work, fear of the dentist. In other words, he uses a *topic sentence*.

Now notice what follows this topic sentence. The speaker illustrates his point. He gives specific details: blue Buick and a yelling man; fenceposts and tractor-driving and blisters; knees turning to water. Then he makes a final statement, bringing his comment to a close. Listen carefully to the conversations that go on around you (or to your own), and you will find this pattern illustrated again and again.

The speaker is quite unaware, of course, that he is following any particular pattern. If you pointed it out to him, he would probably look at you in astonishment and say, "You're crazy. That's just the natural way to talk." Which, of course, it is.

It is also the natural way to write paragraphs. The pattern, or structure, is exactly the same. State your point. Explain or illustrate your point. Conclude. The pattern is identical, whether you are talking or writing. You use the pattern every day in conversation without knowing you use it. Start using it consciously in your writing, and paragraphing will cease to be a mystery.

Your writing, of course, will have a different tone from your ordinary speech, for you aren't chattering with a friend when you write—you are putting yourself on record for the whole educated community. So you will select your details with greater care and draw upon a richer vocabulary than you ordinarily use in conversation. Your tone will be informal but not careless and slangy—slang can often be effective in speech, but it usually sounds puerile in writing. Ideally, your tone should be informed, intelligent, and friendly.

The pattern is the same one you use in speech: topic sentence, explanation and illustration, conclusion.

Picture-Frame Paragraphs

The paragraph pattern will be very easy to master if you force yourself to *visualize* what you want to say in those middle sentences. Write your topic sentence, then ask yourself what kind of photograph you would take, or what kind of picture you would paint, to illustrate your point. Give yourself time to see this picture clearly in your own mind. Then put the picture into words, using detail as a photographer or a painter would use it.

The result will be a vivid picture framed between the topic sentence and the concluding sentence. Your reader will *see* what you mean. You are showing him, not telling him.

The practice of using specific illustrations and vivid detail, of showing rather than telling, is perhaps the most important difference between interesting and uninteresting writing:

> The children of Harlem are born into a world that few white children ever encounter. They live in terrible poverty. They do not have the advantages that other children accept as a matter of course.

You can read that without any real stir of interest. It tells but it does not show. But supply the reader with pictures, and interest goes up immediately:

> The Harlem child is born into a world that few white children ever encounter. He lives in a crowded coldwater flat, a place of peeling wallpaper and crumbling plaster and the ugly, scuttling sound of rats.

Notice that the word "poverty" does not even appear in the second example, yet unquestionably the *effect* of poverty is greater. You no longer have the vaguely general term, "poverty." You have a *picture*. The writer becomes a cameraman, recording the actual details that add up to something far more convincing than any abstract word.

Notice also that the topic sentence has undergone a slight change, from "children of Harlem" to "Harlem child." The effect of this is to increase dramatic impact; the writer moves in, just as a motion-picture cameraman moves in, for a close-up shot. One deprived child, seen as an individual, is far more real and dramatic to the reader than any generalization about "children."

The more color, sound, and movement that you can work into your middle sentences, the more convincing your picture will be. This is true even with essentially undramatic material. For example, one writer might describe a winter day like this:

> It was very cold. It was so cold that nobody wanted to stay outside. Everybody found this kind of weather very uncomfortable.

Another writer, with a better eye for detail, might put it this way:

> It was very cold, so cold that the atmosphere itself seemed almost solid. The sidewalks were ridged and lumpy with caked ice, and the dirty crystals of old gray snow crunched underfoot with a dry, splintering sound. The trees were bare black skeletons, their branches like outstretched arms frozen into gestures of dismay. In the play-

ground a deserted sled lay on its back like some great sprawled insect, its runners coated with ice. Even children stayed indoors on a day like this. It was too cold to play.

The first paragraph *tells* the reader; the second paragraph *shows* him. It is hardly necessary to point out which is more effective.

In paragraphs that must carry some main line of argument, the picture-frame technique will vary somewhat. If your thesis, for example, is "Typing should be a required course," and your topic sentence is "The student should be required to type every paper he hands in," you might have a paragraph like this:

The student should be required to type every paper he hands in, particularly for English class. This would not only conserve the eyesight and sweeten the disposition of his teacher—it would help the student learn. No longer able to hide his spelling errors behind blots and erasures and unrecognizable squiggles, he will learn to spell better. Unable to fatten his essays simply by enlarging his handwriting, he will be forced to come up with some real ideas. And he will be less likely to dash off just any kind of nonsense in order to fill up space; silly statements have a way of looking very silly indeed, even to their author, when they are neatly lined up in precise and impersonal black type. The student can see his own errors with a new and painful clarity, thus becoming both a better writer and a better student.

Note that in this case the topic sentence represents a clear line of argument ("The student should be required . . ."), and thus presents a somewhat different problem from the paragraphs on pages 76–77, in which the topic sentences are primarily statements of fact ("The Harlem child is born . . .", "It was very cold . . ."). An argumentative topic sentence requires more than pictorial detail; it must be supported by concrete examples to back up the *why* as well as the *what* of its statement.

That word "concrete" is important. Concrete means real, specific, actual. To recognize the importance of concreteness, you need only see what would happen to the paragraph above if all the specific detail were removed:

The student should be required to type all his papers. This would make for easier grading. It would also lead to a general improvement in all the student's written work. . . .

The passage is not only less interesting but also less convincing. The two go together. If you want to interest a reader, use concrete examples full of specific details. In other words, don't just tell him. *Show* him.

Summary

The middle paragraphs of an essay constitute your "body of argument," and the number of paragraphs you write for any essay depends upon the number of points you want to make. The length of these paragraphs can vary enormously, but for the time being you should concentrate on writing fairly long paragraphs in order to get a firm sense of their structure: a beginning, a middle, and an end.

The easiest way to master this structure is by visualizing what you are writing about. *See* what you mean, then *show* your reader what you see, in a picture-frame paragraph—a paragraph in which the topic sentence and the concluding sentence act as a frame for a picture made vivid in your middle sentences with specific details.

Everything you write about will seem more real, both to you and to your reader, when you master the picture-frame technique. And you will find, as you move from point to point, explaining and illustrating as you go, that paragraphing has become a simple and quite natural process.

QUESTIONS

1. How does the structure of a middle paragraph differ from the structure of an introductory paragraph? From that of a concluding paragraph?
2. What is the main purpose of paragraphing?
3. Students of composition are advised to write "big" paragraphs while they are learning. Why?
4. In what way does the structure of a paragraph resemble the structure of a full essay?
5. What is the function of the first sentence in a paragraph? What is this sentence called?
6. What is the function of the middle section of a paragraph?
7. Why does the three-part paragraph structure automatically insure the "one point, one paragraph" rule?

8. How does paragraph structure resemble conversation? In what way will it differ?
9. Explain the "picture-frame paragraph." Is this different from basic paragraph structure, or is it simply another way of describing the structure?
10. The picture-frame paragraph that is primarily descriptive will differ somewhat from one that is argumentative. How?
11. Analyze the following paragraph. What major rule of paragraph structure does it violate?

> The old-fashioned American kitchen was the living center of the American home. That was where the family ate its meals, where children studied and women sewed and men read the newspaper, where every family crisis was settled. It was a big, warm, cluttered place, full of all the smells that meant home—freshly baked bread and starched curtains and stick cinnamon and scrubbed linoleum and apples and oilcloth. The kitchen was really the *living* room—the place where the family lived. The mothers in those days did not usually hold jobs outside the home. Unfortunately, today's modern industrial society has taken women away from their homes.

ASSIGNMENT

1. Write a paragraph (using correct paragraph structure) explaining what is wrong with the following paragraph. Be explicit.

> Too many students believe that popularity depends not upon what they are but upon what they have. They want their parents to buy them all the things that they feel will guarantee popularity. They feel that these things will solve all their problems and make them happy. This may affect their personalities in a very bad way.

2. Rewrite the above paragraph, using the picture-frame technique.
3. Write a paragraph that is primarily descriptive, beginning with this topic sentence: "The day was wet and rainy."
4. Write a paragraph that is primarily argumentative, beginning with this topic sentence: "Few girls are really interested in athletic events."
5. Write a paragraph about some television show that you particularly like or dislike. Remember, you cannot use *I, me, my, mine, you,* or *your.* Try to make your opinion clear to the reader by means of descriptive detail.

VOCABULARY

1. Write a definition for each of the following words:

graphic	predetermine	visualize
ingenuity	puerile	willy-nilly
	rhetorical	

2. Finish each of the unfinished sentences below, so that it will demonstrate your understanding of the meaning of the italicized word:

   a. Her description of the thief was *graphic*. She made us see him as a.................................... in ...., with....................... and with ....
   b. She had shown a great deal of *ingenuity* in making her costume for the party. She had......................... ....
   c. You can't *predetermine* the length of any paragraph because, in the course of writing it, ...
   d. Most of his attempts to prove his sophistication are *puerile*—for example, his habit of...................
   e. Don't give me *rhetorical* answers. Give me an answer that tells me ....
   f. The boy had never been to the small town where his father had grown up, but he could *visualize* it. He thought of it as................... (use several details)
   g. It seemed to her that she had spent her entire life doing what other people told her to do, *willy-nilly*. She wished that, just once, she could..............................

7

Connections Between Paragraphs

In Chapter 6 you took a close look at the paragraph to see how it was made, examining it apart from the whole essay just as you might examine a carburetor apart from an engine or a single musical phrase apart from a whole composition.

You found that the paragraph has a certain wholeness or independence of its own; it could stand alone and still make sense.

You must remember, however, that no matter how well a paragraph stands alone it is always just one small part of a larger whole—the essay itself. And in order to do its part in the whole operation, it must connect smoothly with the parts around it. Like a loaded car on a moving freight train, it carries its own separate portion of cargo, but it must be firmly coupled to the car immediately ahead.

As a matter of fact, it might not be a bad idea to think of your essay as a moving train. Your introduction is the locomotive; it commands a clear view of the track, gives a warning toot to announce its departure, and supplies the power to set all the wheels in motion. The body of your essay is the string of paragraphs behind that locomotive, each one a freight car with its particular load of thought. And your conclusion, of course, is the caboose—the little car on the end commanding a view of the country just passed through.

One thing this analogy should make clear is that all those separate cars, if they are to reach their destination, must be firmly hitched together. (If they weren't, you might wind up with a locomotive in Chicago, a string of freight cars scattered over the landscape all the way from Bangor to Tallahassee, and a caboose left sitting high and dry on a siding.) In exactly the same way, your essay can fall apart disastrously unless your paragraphs are firmly linked together.

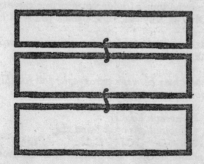

Figure 8—Connections Between Paragraphs

A single example should make this abundantly clear. Below are two "unhitched" paragraphs from a typical student essay:

Girls spend far too much time in front of a mirror. They seem to spend at least half their waking hours examining their pores or brushing their eyelashes or adjusting a curl over their right ear to an exact 45-degree angle. They primp constantly.

Girls tend to be good students. They do their assignments faithfully and neatly, organize their work well, and maintain consistently high grades.   *

The two paragraphs seem to have no relation at all to each other. Bewildered, the reader looks for a connection. Could these two paragraphs possibly have come one after the other in the same essay? The answer is yes—provided they were properly linked:

> *Primp as they may, however,* girls tend to be good students. . . .

Begin the second paragraph like that, and the reader follows the train of thought without the slightest difficulty. *Primp as they may, however,* cues him in. Girls have their faults, and nobody can resist needling them a little, but (and here the reader is comfortably at home again with the real thesis) girls manage to be good students, in spite of their faults.

These links between paragraphs are called *transitions,* or *transitional devices.* They have one purpose: to help the reader follow a main line of thought. As the writer, you know exactly what you have in mind each time you make a shift in meaning. But you can't expect your reader to know: he can't read your mind or hear the tone of your voice or see the expression on your face. He can only catch the signals you send him through words.

He needs, in short, a clear transition—a word or phrase that will link the paragraphs together for him.

> *Transitions between paragraphs fall roughly into three categories:*
> 1. *Standard devices*
> 2. *Paragraph hooks*
> 3. *Combinations of #1 and #2*

The standard devices are simple and obvious; they are specific words and phrases, and using them is hardly more than a matter of selection. The paragraph hooks are more sophisticated—and more fun. And when you have mastered the technique of the hook, the combinations will come easily and naturally. No one of the three is "better" than the others; they are all useful and necessary.

The wise writer will make use of all of them.

Standard Devices

Perhaps you have already noticed that certain words and phrases recur often in your writing as you develop a thesis. If you want to acknowledge a point that isn't debatable, you may write "It is true that . . ." or "Admittedly," or "Obviously," or any one of several similar expressions. These are the *con* transitions, notifying the reader that you intend to concede a point. A few sentences later you will come back with a "Nevertheless," or "But . . ." that clearly signals your intention to present arguments in your favor.

Such words and phrases are among the standard transitional devices for leading your reader through an argument. They notify him briefly and efficiently that conflicting points of view are being presented; without them, as you saw in the example on page 82, the conflicting statements seem quite irrational. Here are a few more examples to illustrate the difficulties you can run into:

> Girls are a nuisance.
> They are wonderful.
>
> The project had value.
> It wasted time.
>
> He was a brilliant actor.
> He often performed miserably.

These paired statements simply don't make sense. Yet the same statements become perfectly clear when they are supplied with transitions:

> *True,* girls are a nuisance.
> *Nevertheless,* they are wonderful.
>
> *Admittedly,* the project had value.
> *But* it was wasted time.
>
> He was, *to be sure,* a brilliant actor.
> *Yet* he often performed miserably.

These examples are, of course, oversimplified in order to emphasize the necessity for proper transition; but if each sentence were a fully developed paragraph, the problem of transition would be the same.

You will be tempted to believe that because a connection between ideas is perfectly clear to you as a writer it is also perfectly clear to the reader. It isn't. The reader needs to be reminded constantly of exactly where you stand. So never omit the transition between paragraphs as you move back and forth between *pro* and *con* arguments.

For additional and more detailed examples of *pro* and *con* transitions, look back at the sample essay structures in Figures 4 and 5, on pages 51–52.

Not all the mechanical transitions, of course, can be classified as strictly *pro* or *con*. What you use, and how you use it, will depend upon the purpose of the paragraph it introduces. You will use one kind of transition when you are shifting your point of view:

> Girls are a *nuisance.*
> *Nevertheless,* they are wonderful.

and another kind when you are simply adding another paragraph in the same vein:

> Girls are a nuisance.
> *Furthermore,* they are gossips.

Other transitional phrases are primarily for emphasis, whether *pro* or *con:*

> Girls are, *in fact,* a menace to society.
> Girls are, *in fact,* the most marvelous creatures in the world.

The best guide to transitions is common sense—and a list like the following. It should give you a word or phrase that will introduce almost any paragraph of argument:

Admittedly	In addition	On the other hand
And	In fact	Still
Assuredly	Indeed	The fact remains
But	It is true that	Therefore
Certainly	Moreover	Thus
Clearly, then	Nevertheless	To be sure
Consequently	No doubt	True
Even so	Nobody denies	Undoubtedly
Furthermore	Obviously	Unquestionably
Granted	Of course	Yet

This is a fairly comprehensive list of standard transitional devices. It is not, however, a complete list. One very important transitional word has been left out—the word "however."

However is such a splendid transition, so useful, so convenient, so downright indispensable—and so often misused—that it needs special treatment.

A NOTE ON "HOWEVER"

The problem with *however* has nothing to do with its meaning. As a transitional device it means exactly the same thing as *but*. But *however* doesn't always sound right. The problem arises from its position in the sentence.

A student writer will almost invariably give *however* first position in a sentence: "*However*, good study habits can't be established overnight." Told not to use first position, he will make a flying leap and deposit it at the end of the sentence: "Good study habits can't be established overnight, *however*."

Nothing is wrong with either of these positions grammatically. But something is wrong with them rhythmically. The best position for *however* is nearly always inside a sentence, between commas:

> Good study habits, *however*, can't be established overnight.

In a compound sentence, it will usually appear inside the first clause:

> Good study habits, *however*, can't be established overnight, and the sooner students learn this the better.

In a complex sentence, it can come either inside the main clause or after the dependent clause, according to the emphasis you prefer:

> Good study habits, *however*, can't be established overnight, as many students learn to their sorrow.

> OR

> As many students learn to their sorrow, *however*, good study habits can't be established overnight.

In any case, *however* works best if it is inside the sentence. Just exactly why this position is best is one of those stylistic mysteries that can't really be explained. It simply sounds better that way. And the importance of sound can't be dismissed, even in silent reading. A reader's inner ear is always cocked and listening, registering every rhythm and cadence of printed language whether that language is spoken aloud or not. And that inner ear likes to have *however* tucked discreetly inside a sentence, usually at one of the following points:

After the subject:

> Electricity, *however*, changed the lives of farmers.
> Driving on the beach, *however*, can be a risky business.

After the predicate:

> They believed, *however*, that right was on their side.
> The bus broke down, *however*, before it reached the school.

After an introductory phrase:

> In many small ways, *however*, the situation had improved.
> After dinner, *however*, they had time to talk.

Note that in all these sentences *however* is protected on each side by a comma. This is the *only* correct punctuation for a tucked-in *however*. Remember that, and you won't make the mistake of trying to use *however* between two independent clauses—a common mistake in student writing. "He was a handsome boy, *however*, he was not very interesting." That doesn't really make sense, as you can see the moment you put in the two commas. So you move your *however* and say what you really mean—thus discovering that you need two separate sentences: "He was a handsome boy. He was not, *however*, very interesting."

Occasionally you will find yourself with a *however* that simply refuses to be tucked into a sentence comfortably. In that case, change it to *but* and put it in first position:

> She wanted to apologize, to explain, to let him know that she was sorry. *But* she was afraid of him.

Try reading these two sentences aloud, using *however* instead of *but*. You will discover that no matter where you put the *however* it will have a flat and stilted sound. In some mysterious way the word *but* (which will work only in first position) immediately gives the sentence a more humane and natural tone.

Nobody can prescribe precisely when to put *but* at the head of a sentence or when to use, instead, a tucked-in *however*.

This is something you must decide on the basis of your own preference. Try them both for size; test them against your inner ear for tone. But don't use one of them exclusively. For the sake of variety, use first one, then the other.

Paragraph Hooks

Although *however* and the other transitional devices listed on page 84 are indispensable to the writer, enabling him to make dozens of connections neatly and efficiently, they can't handle the whole transitional load. Even if they could, no writer would depend upon them exclusively, for they can become painfully obvious when they are used over and over again. You want your reader to be pleasantly aware that your paragraphs are firmly linked, but you don't want him to see the chains too clearly or hear them clank too audibly into place.

So you need another kind of transition, something that is both stronger and subtler. You have it in the *paragraph hook*.

You probably use the paragraph hook often in your own writing without knowing it and see it constantly in your reading without realizing it (as in this sentence, for example). But to take full advantage of its possibilities, you should learn to use the paragraph hook consciously, to direct and control it for your own purposes. Control, remember, is the essence of style, and the handling of transitions is an important part of any writer's style.

To see how the paragraph hook differs from the standard transitional device, look first at the example below. Here the transition from one paragraph to the next is accomplished by a standard transition alone—the word *but:*

> Mark Twain is established in the minds of most Americans as a kindly humorist, a gentle and delightful "funny man." No doubt his photographs have helped promote this image. Everybody is familiar with the Twain face. He looks like every child's ideal grandfather, a dear old white-thatched gentleman who embodies the very spirit of loving-kindness.

(Standard transition)

> *But* Twain wrote some of the most savage satire ever produced in America. . . .

The standard transition indicates clearly enough that the writer is preparing to take off with a new idea in opposition to the one in the first paragraph. But the transition is far too abrupt. The leap from one idea (how Twain looked) to the next (how he wrote) is simply too great to be handled by a mechanical transition. Observe how much more firmly the paragraphs hang together if the transition is made like this:

.............................., a dear old white-thatched gentleman who embodies the very spirit of loving-kindness.

(Paragraph hook)

    The *loving-kindness* begins to look a little doubtful in view of some of his writing. For Twain wrote some of the most savage satire . . .

Here you see demonstrated the simplest kind of paragraph hook. The last word of the first paragraph is hooked into the first sentence of the second paragraph and used as a point of departure for introducing another idea. This repetition hooks the paragraphs together solidly. The hook need not be one word; it can be a phrase. It should not, however, exceed two or three words.

Although the last word or phrase of a paragraph frequently serves as the simplest and strongest kind of hook, you can go back farther than this, sometimes to even better effect:

.............................., a dear old white-thatched gentleman who embodies the very spirit of loving-kindness.

(Deeper hook)

    This *dear old white-thatched gentleman* happens to be the author of some of the most savage satire . . .

Generally speaking, the last sentence of a paragraph is the best place to find the hook for your new paragraph, for this sentence is the one freshest in the reader's mind. If you go back much deeper than this, you will usually need a multiple hook, as in this example:

...................No doubt his photographs have helped promote this image. . . . He looks like . . . the very spirit of loving-kindness.

(Still deeper: the multiple hook)

> To accept such an *image* is to betray greater familiarity
> with the *photographs* than with the writing. For Twain
> wrote some of the most savage satire . . .

Here both *image* and *photographs* are repeated, thus
"double hooking" the paragraphs to make up for the greater
distance between their first and second appearance. The
greater the distance, the more likely you are to need a multiple hook. But no arbitrary rule in this matter is possible.
Let your inner ear and your good sense guide you. The important thing is to remember the reader. Make certain that
the connection is clear to him. But don't insult him by making
the connection *too* clear—that is, by repeating huge sections
or whole sentences from the preceding paragraph. One or two
key words will do the job.

All the examples so far have been simple word or phrase
hooks. Another variation of the paragraph hook is the *idea
hook*. The principle is the same; you hook into the preceding
paragraph, but instead of repeating an exact word or phrase
you refer to the idea just expressed, compressing it into a
single phrase:

> Mark Twain is . . . .
> . . . . the very spirit of loving-kindness.

(Idea hook)

> *Such a view* of Twain would probably have been a
> source of high amusement to the author himself. For
> Twain wrote some of the most savage satire . . .

or

> Any resemblance between *this popular portrait* and the
> man who reveals himself in his writing is purely imaginary.
> For Twain wrote . . .

In neither of the above examples is an exact word or phrase
from the first paragraph repeated. But the hook is clearly
there; the referential *such a view* and *this popular portrait*
fasten the paragraphs firmly together.

The idea hook can be a great deal more subtle than this,
of course. If you examine the work of any accomplished
essayist you will find many paragraphs that have no specific
word or phrase serving as a link but that are nevertheless unmistakably tied together by meaning. Transitions of this kind
require some of the subtlest skills of writing—the ordering
of ideas, the use of inference and allusion, the creation of
"echo effects," the unobtrusive handling of time and empha-

sis. All these are skills that derive from an intimate understanding of language—and from experience.

That takes time. Meanwhile the simple idea hook illustrated above can serve you well. By using it you can avoid the danger of overloading your work with either the word hooks or the purely mechanical transitions. Any transitional method, remember, can become annoyingly obvious to a reader if it is overused. So vary your practice, never permitting one method of handling transitions to take over the job exclusively.

The Combinations

The combination of standard transitions and paragraph hooks is so natural that you will probably find yourself using it as a matter of course. Any of the samples provided on pages 87–89, for example, could be used to demonstrate combinations:

> The *loving-kindness* begins to look a little doubtful, *however,* in view of . . .
> *Yet* this *dear old white-thatched gentleman* . . .
> *But* to accept such an *image* . . .
> *Such a view* of Twain, *however,* would probably . . .

Whether or not to use a single transition or a combination depends partly upon your sense of what the reader requires for clarity and partly upon your own view of your material and your natural rhythm in writing. If you are certain that you have made yourself perfectly clear with a single transition, let it stand. If you are not certain, or if the rhythm of the sentence seems to need an extra beat, use the combination.

Summary

Remember that the chief purpose of transitions is to help your reader follow your train of thought. They are the links that hold your ideas together and keep them moving toward a single goal. So make certain, always, that some kind of link exists between your paragraphs, and that the link exists not only in your own mind but also, clearly and unmistakably, in the words you put on paper.

One kind of link is not necessarily better than any other kind, but variety is better than sameness. So try for variety. Use the purely mechanical devices for quick and simple transitions. Use word and phrase hooks for stronger and clearer links. Use idea hooks for broad references. Use combinations for emphasis and tone.

Use them all. But above all, use them. -

QUESTIONS

1. If a paragraph can stand alone as a structure, why should it need to be linked to any other paragraph?
2. Explain the analogy between an essay and a moving train.
3. What are the three kinds of transitions that link paragraphs?
4. Describe a standard transitional device. Give examples.
5. When *however* is used as a transition, what is the best position for it in the sentence?
6. What is the correct punctuation for a tucked-in *however*?
7. This sentence appears on page 87: "You probably use the paragraph hook often in your own writing without knowing it and see it constantly in your reading without realizing it (as in this sentence, for example)." What is the paragraph hook in this sentence? You will have to look back to the paragraph preceding the sentence for your answer.
8. Describe the difference between a simple paragraph hook and a deeper hook.
9. What is a multiple hook?
10. How does an idea hook differ from the other kinds of paragraph hooks?
11. What is a combination hook?
12. Is one kind of transition better than any other kind? If so, why? If not, what is the best guide for deciding which kind of transition to use after you have made certain that you are being clear?

ASSIGNMENT

1. Assume that each of the paired sentences below is the first sentence of two consecutive paragraphs. Supply a transition for the second sentence of each pair:

a. He received the highest praise for his efforts to improve living conditions in the slums.
   He was frequently criticized.

    b. The study of science can be a tremendously exciting
        intellectual experience.
        The study of science can have a narrowing effect.

    c. She caused trouble wherever she went.
        She was the kind of woman who could turn a peaceful
        exchange of views on the weather into a war of nerves.

    d. Students are showing greater interest in baseball as a
        school sport.
        Students are showing a greater interest in dramatics.

    e. The furniture he had acquired for his living room was
        surely as ugly as anything ever made by man.
        It was comfortable.

    f. Far too much emphasis has been placed on psychology
        and too little on personal responsibility.
        A knowledge of psychology can be very valuable.

    g. The movie was the victim of poor photography and a
        bad script.
        It was interesting.

2. Insert the word *however* in the second sentence of each
    pair below:

    a. He had taken piano lessons for ten years.
        He was not a good pianist.

    b. She planned to finish the assignment on Monday.
        By Monday she had forgotten all about it.

    c. She had very few interests that could be called hobbies.
        She liked to take long walks in the city, and these led
        her eventually to make the city itself her hobby.

    d. The council has adopted a "wait and see" attitude.
        This is no solution.

3. Write a picture-frame paragraph in which you describe
    some aspect of your trip to school each morning—perhaps
    a single city block where you walk, the bus ride through
    a particular section of town or country, or the attitude of
    other students you encounter. Then do the following:

    a. Write the first sentence of the next paragraph, using a
        paragraph hook. (You may also include a standard
        device if you like.)

    b. Write another first sentence for your second paragraph,
        using a deeper hook.

    c. Write another first sentence, using a multiple hook.

    d. Write another first sentence, using an idea hook.

    e. Write a full paragraph, using one of the sentences above
        as your opening sentence. This will give you two full
        paragraphs.

    f. Write the opening sentence of a third paragraph to fol-
low the two you have just written, using a combination
hook for the transition.

VOCABULARY

1. Write a definition for each of the following words:

analogy	discreetly	recur
appropriate*	indispensable	referential
arbitrary	irrational	sophisticated
	multiple	

2. In the left-hand column below are different forms of the
words in the vocabulary list. Write a complete sentence in
which you use each of these words and also *all* the words
and/or phrases that appear opposite it in the right-hand
column. This will require a little inventiveness on your
part. Your sentence may be as long as you like, and you
can fit the combinations into your sentence in any way you
please, but hold yourself to one sentence in each case.

a.	analogous	links between paragraphs
b.	appropriately	class, subdued
c.	arbitrarily	time, limited
d.	discreet	information, questions
e.	discretion	allowed, choice
f.	dispense	formality, point
g.	irrationally	convinced, plotting to
h.	multiplying	troubles, blamed, carelessness
i.	recurrent	dream, pursued, who wanted to
j.	reference	understand, background
k.	referring	notes, the impression that
l.	sophistication	dress, contrast, naturalness

8

The Passive Voice

In this age of the club and the committee, you have probably
listened (or more likely, not listened) at some time in your
life to something like this: "The meeting was called to order

---

    * This word has two different meanings and two different pronuncia-
tions. Consult your dictionary.

by the president. The minutes were read. The treasurer's report was given. . . ." And so forth, and so forth, and so forth.

No doubt at this very moment thousands of people, all of them glassy-eyed with boredom, are sitting in a meeting somewhere and listening to a duly-elected secretary read words very much like these. Most of them, including the secretaries, would agree that the minutes of meetings can easily win any contest for the World's Dullest Writing.

Nobody blames the secretaries: they are simply the victims of a style that has solidified into a convention. Any attempt to change the custom would probably panic the membership. Nor can the meetings themselves be blamed. Sometimes they're interesting. But by the time the proceedings have been put through the minutes-machine, all the interest has been efficiently and thoroughly removed. Even if something really memorable should happen—if an escaped lion, say, should stroll into a committee meeting—the minutes would probably record the event like this:

> The meeting was interrupted by the appearance of a lion. An attempt was made to form a barricade with the furniture. Members were told to remain calm. The police were called. . . .

If you happened to be present at such a meeting, if you had actually found yourself eyeball to eyeball with an uncaged lion, a lion quite possibly on the verge of selecting you for his afternoon snack, you might find this version of the episode a shade inadequate to express your own feelings at the time. You feel cheated. Judging by those minutes, you tell a friend resentfully, you'd think nothing at all had happened. A bunch of words has turned something real into something unreal.

Why? How did it happen? What was wrong with the words?

The answer to that question will give you the key to the biggest single problem that faces you as a writer.

Glance again at those sample minutes. They lack suspense, of course, and the kind of detail that helps establish the look and feel of a situation. But something more basic than this is involved; suspense and detail can be added later, after you have located the real trouble. Go straight to the heart of the sentences. Examine the verbs: *was called, were read, was given; was interrupted, was made, were told, were called.* Can these verbs be responsible for the lifelessness, the pervasive dullness, the unrealness of the writing?

They can be, and they are. At bottom, the sentences are

lifeless because the verbs are lifeless. And they are lifeless because *they are all in passive voice.*

What It Is, and How to Beat It

The English language has two voices—active voice and passive voice. These terms refer to the use of verbs. Most verbs can be either active or passive, depending upon how you use them. Active voice is direct, vigorous, strong; passive voice is indirect, limp, weak—and sneaky. It can creep unnoticed into your writing unless you are on guard against it constantly and consciously. It is every student's worst enemy, mainly because he does not recognize it and thus has no defense against it. So you must learn quickly and forever the difference between the two voices. All your progress from this point forward may depend upon your understanding of this difference. It is that important.

The difference can be quickly and simply illustrated:

Active voice: John drove the car.

John is the subject of the sentence, and John *acted.* He did something—he *drove.* The verb shows him in action. Any other sentence with an active verb could demonstrate the same principle: "John likes Mary. Bells rang. The teacher called the roll. My feet hurt." Whenever a verb shows the subject of a sentence *doing something,* the sentence is in active voice.

Now see the contrast:

Passive voice: The car was driven by John.

In this sentence, the subject is *car.* But notice that the car is doing nothing whatever—*it is having something done to it.* You had exactly the same situation in the record of the lion episode: "The meeting was interrupted . . . An attempt was made . . . Members were told . . ." The subjects did not act; they were *acted upon.* Whenever this happens, the sentence is in passive voice.

Perhaps you can see what an extraordinary difference voice can make in style by looking at two versions of a longer sentence:

> Bells were rung, horns were blown, confetti was thrown from every office window, and embraces were exchanged by total strangers.

> Bells rang, horns tooted, confetti streamed from every office window, and total strangers threw their arms around each other.

Both sentences say exactly the same thing, but the second version is unquestionably livelier and more interesting than the first. Voice, of course, makes all the difference.

Adrift in Nobody-Land

The chief weakness of passive voice is its anonymity. It could almost be called the "nobody" voice:

> The room was cleaned.
> The flowers were cut.
> The lights were turned on.

Who cleaned the room? Who cut the flowers? Who turned on the lights? Who, indeed? Apparently nobody. Ghostly hands have been at work. Everything has taken place in a vacuum; the events seem unreal and shadowy because they lack any sense of human involvement.

This "nobodiness" usually gets through even to the habitual user of passive voice. He begins to sense that something is missing, so he hitches a body to the end of the sentence:

> The room was cleaned by Mary.
> The flowers were cut by Josephine.
> The lights were turned on by Pearlie May.

That may help his conscience, but it doesn't help his writing. Attaching a live body to an inert, lethargic verb is like putting a rider on a doped horse. The horse—or the sentence—still won't move. You will notice that in spite of the "by —" phrase added to the sentences above, the subjects still haven't moved an inch. Not one of them is acting; each is still being acted upon. It just sits there and lets things happen to it, meekly accepting whatever the rest of the sentence chooses to dish out.

In real life we are bored and exasperated by passivity. When we come into contact with apathetic, characterless people who limply allow themselves to be pushed around, who never make a decision, never respond, never take the initiative, we feel like giving them a good shaking. Complete passivity is unnatural; it offends some basic sense of life in all of us, some insistent demand for human statement and identity.

What bores us in real life bores us no less in writing. And

although good manners usually prevent us from shaking some life into passive, listless acquaintances, politeness need not deter us from shaking up our own sentences. In fact, one good way to handle a sentence suffering from passive voice is to cut off its tail and switch it around entirely:

> *Not:* The room was cleaned by Mary.
> *But:* Mary cleaned the room.
>
> *Not:* The flowers were cut by Josephine.
> *But:* Josephine cut the flowers.
>
> *Not:* The lights were turned on by Pearlie May.
> *But:* Pearlie May turned on the lights.

Notice that the word "by" simply disappears. This minor operation is the simplest and easiest way to get rid of passive voice. Always be suspicious of a two-part verb that is followed by a "by —" phrase. (All passive verbs, incidentally, have two parts.) The "by —" phrase is harmless if it indicates time or place ("I'll be finished by noon." "I went by the path."), but if it means *done by*, it's a dead giveaway of passive voice. Hack it off, change the subject of the sentence, and let the "by —" disappear forever.

Making the Subject Perform

It is not always practical to get rid of passive voice by changing the subject of a sentence. "Thunder was heard in the mountains," for example, has no "by —" phrase. And it would be absurd to add one just so that you could switch it forward; the result would be something vague and unsatisfactory like "Everybody heard thunder in the mountains" or "Many people heard . . ." The important thing in the sentence is the thunder itself, not who heard it. So leave it where it is. But make it *do* something:

> Thunder *growled* in the mountains.

Now it's in action. It's doing the thing that thunder does. It could also *grumble,* or *mutter,* or *rumble,* or *crash,* or *complain,* or *snarl,* depending upon the kind of thunder-sound you want. The more precise the verb, the more vivid and real the subject becomes. No reader cares in the least about thunder that "was heard." It's the thunder he hears himself that makes him jump. And an active verb gives it to him straight; thunder that grumbles or snarls is real thunder.

Don't let passive voice steal your thunder. Don't let it steal even the smallest sound. Sound is a sign of life and movement. Transmit it with an active verb:

> Passive: The sound of dishwashing was heard.
> Active: Dishes clattered in the sink.
>
> Passive: The door was shut with great force.
> Active: The door slammed.
>
> Passive: The motor was turned on.
> Active: The motor coughed into life.
>
> Passive: The room was filled with the sudden sound of laughter.
> Active: The room exploded with laughter.

Whenever you can create sound with an active verb, your writing will immediately take on a new and lively sense of reality. Take advantage of these "audio active" verbs whenever possible.

The most powerful of all the active verbs, however, are those that create pictures in a reader's mind. One verb can often bring a whole scene to life, complete with sound track. Consider, for example, this limply passive sentence: "The car was driven down Main Street." You can put the sentence in active voice easily enough by changing the verb to *went*, but that verb is so low-voltage that it's only a step removed from passivity. Make your reader *see* that car; pack a moving picture into your verb:

> The car careened down Main Street.

Instantly the car comes into focus. It is no longer merely "going" down Main Street; it is lurching crazily from side to side.

"The car jolted down Main Street" supplies a different picture and new information; either the car has a flat or Main Street needs a new paving job. "The car steamed down Main Street" shows us a hissing and sputtering car, with a white plume of vapor erupting from its radiator.

The writer need only pick the verb that paints the picture in his mind. Maybe the car *rattled* down Main Street. Or *purred*. Or *whispered*. If the car rattles, it's old and ramshackle and probably ready to fall apart. If it purrs, it is probably new and quite expensive. If it whispers, it is very expensive indeed—a Rolls Royce, perhaps, gleaming black, with a uniformed chauffeur in the front seat and a rich old lady in back. She has come into town to buy fresh liver for her cat.

Such is the power of the active verb to tease and please the imagination. The more precisely active the verb, the more vivid the picture it creates. The more vivid the picture, the more effective the writing.

Make your subject do something.

That's the rule to remember. It will put you into active voice, and from that point forward you should experience a steady improvement in style. You will find that by forcing a subject to act you will loosen your imagination and bring verbs to mind that would never have occurred to you before. Your writing will begin to take on some of the power and excitement of direct experience.

That's the highest goal any writer can hope to achieve.

Why Passive Voice at All?

If passive voice is such a menace to style, why not outlaw it altogether? Unfortunately, that's not possible. It's the beginning writer's worst enemy, but it does perform certain functions—limited, but necessary.

Sometimes only passive voice can provide a necessary tone or connotation. It is possible for a verb to be too brisk, too energetic, to express accurately an exact shade of meaning. Or you may feel that a long series of sentences in active voice needs a subtle change in key, a note of softness and distance, simply for contrast. But don't depend entirely on instinct. Try every possible alternative to passive voice first. If active voice simply will not work, if you cannot possibly achieve with it the tone or meaning you want, then passive voice is probably right for your purpose.

But look out for tricks. Look out especially for tricking yourself. You will often be tempted to use passive voice because it sounds pretty or because it's easier. The passive voice sings a siren song. You'll find yourself praising and defending it at the very moment it is leading you toward the rocks.

In only one respect can passive voice be of positive value: its very impersonality has a peculiar and special power. Oddly, this meek and colorless voice often provides exactly the right tone for violence and disaster and accident—for any event in which the subject suffers misfortune. *She was hit by a car*, for example, certainly conveys the sense of real accident, of the victim's helplessness. *A car hit her* does not; put that way, in fact, it sounds almost absurd. Instinctively, we put disaster in passive voice. The wounded soldier looks at his bleeding arm and says, "I've been hit." When we speak of the man in front of the firing squad, we say he *was shot;* the woman in the burning building *was trapped;* the gangster *was taken* for a ride; the child *was kidnapped.* In each instance the passive voice makes it brutally clear that the subject is not acting but is being acted upon. That, of course, is precisely the effect the writer wants: it carries a sense of shock, of helplessness in the face of calamity.

Occasionally you will find it necessary to use the passive voice for the sake of clarity or to achieve a needed change of tone. In the main, however, passive voice is weak and undesirable. Worse yet, it is habit-forming. Avoid it whenever possible.

A Plan for Self-Protection

The best way to avoid passive voice, yet still have it on hand when absolutely necessary, is to follow these five steps:

1. As soon as you pick the subject of a sentence, supply it with a verb that makes it *do* something. Never mind about the rest of the sentence; first get that verb. If you don't write it in passive voice, you won't have to change it. (The is known as the cut-it-off at the-pass technique.)
2. If you use a passive verb, try to change it.
3. If you can't change it, try a new sentence.
4. If that doesn't work, try skipping the sentence altogether.
5. As a last resort, use passive voice.

But keep your guard up. Passive voice can slip into a sentence so smoothly that you never see it enter. If you start looking for it, it melts into the background. If you find it, it has a way of looking touchingly innocent, thus persuading you to leave it alone. Don't be fooled. Get rid of it.

One final warning: the passive voice has two extremes. At one end is secretarial prose. That's the easiest one to fight because it's so obvious. At the other end is a kind of prose perhaps best classified as vaguely poetic. At this extreme, passive voice acquires a peculiar aura of its own, a subtle undertone of ah-how-sweet-and-sad-and-strange the world is (always pleasing to the young, and to the young writer almost irresistible). Resist it. It's just secretarial prose with its face painted, all dressed up but still going nowhere.

Summary

Training yourself to spot the passive voice in your writing and to put it to rout can be an immensely valuable discipline. It will push you not only toward more direct and forceful statement but will give you a sharper awareness of language as a flexible instrument, a thing of movable parts that responds to experiment, adjusts to new patterns. Above all, an attack on passive voice will open up vast new resources of power available in active verbs.

Passive voice will always have certain important uses, but remember that you must keep your eye on it all the time or it will drop its *o* and change swiftly from passive voice to passive vice. You must learn to outwit it. *Make your subject perform.* Adopt that as your guiding principle, and you can vanquish one of your most insidious enemies. Only after you have conquered passive voice can you return to it with confidence, knowing when to use it—and why.

So discipline yourself. Put a deliberate check on your tendency to drift into the passive. Experiment with new arrangements of words. Reach for the precise and vivid verb. Make those sentences move. Then you can be sure they are alive.

QUESTIONS

1. How does the relationship between subject and verb differ in active and passive voice? Give examples.
2. What is meant by the phrase, "a style that has solidified into a convention"?
3. Why is a "by —" phrase frequently a sign of passive voice?
4. How can you convert a sentence containing a "by —" phrase from passive to active voice?
5. What is an "audio-active" verb? Give an example not taken from this chapter.
6. According to an old Chinese proverb, one picture is worth more than ten thousand words. How could you apply this proverb to writing?

7. What one rule will help you to avoid passive voice?
8. Under what circumstances is passive voice more effective than active voice?
9. What is the "cut-it-off-at-the-pass" technique in reference to passive voice?
10. What is meant by the statement that vaguely poetic prose in passive voice "is just secretarial prose with its face painted, all dressed up but still going nowhere"?

ASSIGNMENT

1. Make a list, in the order of their appearance, of all the passive verbs in the following paragraph:

> A man was seen at the intersection, calmly crossing against the light. Cars were brought to a shrieking halt. Horns were honked. Warnings were shouted by the crowd waiting on the corner, and in the distance a series of small crashes could be heard from the growing line of cars as bumpers were engaged unexpectedly. None of this was noticed by the man, a narrow-chested little fellow in a black suit. A black briefcase was carried in one hand and a rolled umbrella in the other. When the opposite side of the intersection was reached, his umbrella was raised in a brief salute to the cars that were now hopelessly stalled for blocks because of him. Then he was seen no more.

2. Rewrite the paragraph in active voice, rearranging the sentences in any way you like to create a smooth sequence.
3. Write an original paragraph describing something you saw yesterday. It can be an event you witnessed or simply an object you observed. It need not be important or exciting, but it must be something real, described as completely as possible. *Use passive voice only.*
4. Rewrite your paragraph in active voice.
5. Write a complete essay with a thesis based on the general subject of passive voice. Make any point you like, but *use the two paragraphs you wrote for #3 and #4 above as examples to illustrate your point.*

VOCABULARY

1. Find a definition for each of the following words:

anonymity	initiative	pervasive
apathetic	irresistible	vacuum
convention	lethargic	vanquish
	memorable	

2. Finish each of the incomplete sentences below, so that it will demonstrate your understanding of the meaning of the italicized word:

    a. On a large college campus a student often suffers from a sense of *anonymity*. He feels that ...., that ...., and that ....
    b. Interest in the athletic program last year was *apathetic* at best. Students either ....or ....
    c. His nominating speech certainly did not follow the standard *convention*. Instead of ...., he........
    d. In the campaign to improve living conditions in the refugee camp, John Fletcher took the *initiative*. He was not the kind of man who could ....
    e. To him the appeal of the sea was *irresistible*. He felt ...., and he ....
    f. He felt completely *lethargic*. He could not ....: what he wanted above all else was ....
    g. It was a *memorable* moment. For the first time in his life he ...., and he knew ....
    h. The peculiar scent in the house, reminiscent of both roses and mildew, was faint but *pervasive*. It clung to ...., emanated from ...., and seemed to be part of ....
    i. The girl's mind seemed to be a complete *vacuum*. She seemed incapable of ...., and she ....
    j. Nothing could *vanquish* his high spirits. Even when ...., he ....

9

The Sound of Sentences

So long ago that you have probably forgotten how or where it happened, you discovered that you could talk—not just pronounce a few words, but string them together and thus express whole thoughts. This miraculous discovery may have taken place very early indeed, perhaps while you were still taking your meals at a highchair and getting things like chopped spinach for lunch—whereupon you probably said, in the manner of any sensible child, "I don't want that spinach. I want candy." If this announcement had no immediate effect on your menu, it at least had dazzling implications for your future. For you were suddenly talking in sentences.

At that age, of course, you had no idea they were called sentences. They were simply sounds—long, satisfying sounds with a solid feeling of beginning, middle, and end. Nobody had to tell you when you had it right. Your own ear took care of that.

Then you learned to read sentences and finally to write them. You may even remember the day you produced your first piece of writing. Clutching a thick lead pencil, perspiring, biting your lower lip, you managed to copy a set of mysterious symbols that spelled out something more or less like this:

> Sally saw the cat.
> It was a big cat.
> It was a black cat.
> It was a big, black cat.

Here, you were told, were Sentences. You had been gabbling happily for several years, of course, in sentences of your own that were far more complicated than these, and certainly more interesting. But you didn't know that. Obviously, if these things on your paper were sentences, then sentences were something entirely different from talk. The proof lay on your desk in front of you: "Sally saw the cat. It was a big cat. It was a black cat . . ." Nobody in his right mind, not even a first-grader, would be caught talking like that.

But you learned, obediently, what you had to learn: that sentences started with a capital letter and ended with a period, that *Sally* was a noun, *saw* was a verb, *big* was an adjective. You probably learned, in addition, a few things that weren't strictly a part of the lesson. You learned to hate Sally. You learned to hate Sally's cat. And you learned to hate sentences. If sentences were this kind of stuff, who wanted them?

Indeed, nobody. But that was something else you couldn't know. So you grew up believing that spoken sentences sounded one way and written sentences another. Written sentences, you were firmly convinced, not only sounded different but were *supposed* to sound different. You learned eventually that some of the things you read seemed almost as easy and natural as talk, but you couldn't quite shake your own sentences free. Sally and that cat were still prowling through your subconscious, putting a stop to any idea you might have of relaxing your guard. You had the uneasy feeling that it was dangerous, even faintly immoral, to put a sentence in writing until you had starched and stiffened and sterilized it beyond any resemblance to natural speech.

That, at any rate, is one theory—a rather playful one, but not altogether unserious—to explain the central problem facing most students in their writing. And that problem is not grammar or spelling or any kind of formal "correctness." These things, to be sure, may be problems, but they are almost entirely separate from the real problem, which is how to write sentences that sound as natural and effortless as talk.

To solve the problem, you must outwit Sally and her cat. You must realize that writing is, in the final analysis, a form of talk—preserved talk, talk that has been caught in flight and pinned down on paper so that the words can be heard again. Heard, mind you—not merely seen. For clinging to every piece of writing is the sound of the writer's voice, the human sound of one person speaking to others. The sound of that voice registers instantly on a reader's inner ear—registers so strongly, in fact, that it is probably true to say that reading is almost as much an act of hearing as of seeing.

When you put a book down because you find it dull or difficult, because you "simply can't read it" or "can't keep your mind on it," it is not your eyes that object to the printed word. It's your ear, objecting to the *sound* of the printed words—that inner ear which demands from all written words the sound of a human voice. It's the same ear that told you, in the first or second grade, that the story of Sally and her cat was a bore. Nobody talked like that, and you knew it.

But if writing should sound like talk, it would appear at first glance very easy to write sentences with the right sound, simply by talking first and writing later—transferring the spoken words to paper exactly as they were spoken. Theoretically, this should result in a sound of absolute naturalness. But here you run into the great paradox of writing:

> *Written sentences should _sound_ like natural speech, but they can't _be_ natural speech.*

The reasons for this are fairly obvious. Natural speech is a great deal more than words. In fact, it depends for most of its effect upon a great number of things that can't be put on paper: tone of voice, facial expressions, gestures, manner, even the speaker's appearance. Strip all these things away—as you must when you transfer spoken language, exactly as spoken, to paper—and the words seem incredibly flat.

In any case, natural speech is far too disorganized, too repetitive, too careless to stand up under the kind of examination it would get in print. Even the most brilliant spoken language tends to flatten into ordinariness when it is converted to written words. So no piece of writing can be defended on the basis of "that's-the-way-I-really-talk." The whole point of writing is to create something a great deal better than you "really" talk—a great deal more interesting, more thoughtful, more effective in every way—but to make it *sound* as natural and effortless as talk.

It begins to look impossible. Your voice, your face, your gestures can't help you. The actual words of speech can't help you. What's left? Only one thing—the *rhythm* of speech. This is the one thing you can borrow from it, the one thing you *must* borrow if your written words are ever to achieve an air of naturalness.

The Rhythm of Speech

All spoken language, no matter who the speaker may be or what his subject is, has a natural rhythm. You will hear this rhythm wherever you hear talk: in your best friend's conversation, in a salesman's pitch, in a math teacher's explanation of a problem, in an impromptu speech at a club meeting, in your father's reading of the riot act.

Compare the two short paragraphs below:

Example A:
I want that car back here by ten o'clock. And when I say ten o'clock, I don't mean ten-thirty or ten-fifteen or ten-five. I mean *ten*. You remember that. Because I'm telling you right now, this is the last time you drive that car if you come home late again. And that's *final*.

Example B:
One of the things that is very important to an actor is a sense of timing. It is more important than a handsome face or a good voice. An actor who does not have a sense of timing can never be very good at acting. A good director can tell him what to do, but he will always be just like a puppet.

As they stand now, the two examples have nothing whatever in common. The first is quite obviously *spoken* language. It's completely natural, but it is certainly not suitable for use in an essay. The second example is quite obviously *not* spoken language; you identify it instantly as a written paragraph, probably from a student essay (which it is). You may feel that the second paragraph is more "dignified" than the first. In any case, the two paragraphs are so completely different

—in approach, in tone, in subject matter—that it would appear impossible to transfer anything at all from one to the other.

Yet something can be transferred. Perhaps you can discover for yourself what it is by examining the paragraph below. It makes exactly the same point it made originally (in Example B, above) but makes it better. And in one respect it is now exactly like Example A. See if you can detect what it is that the two paragraphs now have in common:

> Few things are so essential to an actor as a sense of timing. Without that, nothing else about him matters very much. He may have a handsome face. He may have a splendid voice. But unless he has an innate sense of timing, the finest director in the world cannot make an actor of him. He can never be more than a puppet.

The meaning of the paragraph has not changed. And certainly it is no less "dignified" than before. But it doesn't take a great ear for language to realize that this second version is far more effective as a piece of writing than the first. It is more effective because *the sentences now have the natural rhythm of speech*. In fact, the rhythm of this paragraph is a deliberate repetition of the rhythm of the father's natural speech.

Make a sentence-by-sentence comparison of *sentence length*. The six sentences in both passages are matched for length. The father's speech happened to fall in a pattern of medium-medium-short-short-long-short, so the second paragraph was matched to that pattern. Both paragraphs could now be "graphed" like this:

The fact that the two passages are now exactly alike in sentence length is unimportant; that was done simply for demonstration purposes. The important thing to remember is that the length of sentences in all speech is always erratic, always changing.

The first principle of rhythm in writing, to capture

*the basic rhythm of speech, is variation of sentence
length.*

Furthermore, the mere act of forcing yourself to vary the
length of sentences will force you simultaneously to change
their structure and therefore their wording—always for the
better. Glance again at the first version of Example B. Notice
that every sentence is almost exactly the same length. And
as frequently happens when length does not vary, almost every
sentence has the same monotonous structure. These are nothing
but Sally-cat sentences, grown up and pretending to be dignified, but nevertheless Sally-cat. And your ear rebels for the
same reason it rebelled in the first grade: nobody talks like
that.

So write with a talking rhythm, varying the length of your
sentences to suit your material. Generally the short, sharp
sentence gives emphasis; the long, involved sentence provides
depth and color. Together with the medium-length sentence
they give writing the tone and rhythm of speech. Put them
in any order you like. Any order is right if it sounds right to
your own inner ear. Write for that ear.

If you find it difficult at first to "hear" your sentences, just
use your eyes. If your sentences are all approximately the
same length, vary them arbitrarily. Cut a sentence down here,
extend another one there, join two together, or split a long
one in half. Gradually you will find your own voice, discover
your own particular rhythm.

Getting Inside the Sentence

So far you have been concerned with the broad rhythms of
sentences, with the effect of varied sentence length on the
essay as a whole. Now it is time to look at individual sentences. For although the first step toward achieving a "talking
rhythm" in writing is through variation in sentence length, a
great deal more is involved than length alone. It is not enough
merely to make a sentence longer or shorter; it must also be
made *better*.

It's a great deal easier to write a good short sentence than
a good long one, of course, for in making it short you will
instinctively cut it down to its most important parts. Take this
example:

In general, it can be said that things have a tendency
to happen this way in a person's own experience.

Chop the undergrowth out of that jungle and you are down to essentials:

> That's life.
> or
> Life is like that.

The real problems begin when you write longer sentences. You can make a sentence longer, after all, simply by adding a few meaningless phrases or by repeating in slightly different words what you have already said. The only thing this does for a dull sentence is to make it duller:

> One of the things that is very important to an actor is a sense of timing, because a sense of timing is something every actor must have.

The sentence is certainly longer (compare it to the original on page 106), but it is now worse than dull—it's downright simple-minded. As a reader, you would conclude either that the writer thought you were a moron or that he was one himself—and neither conclusion would make you feel very friendly.

You can, of course, make a sentence longer simply by joining it to another sentence with a connective word. Sometimes this works. But very often it doesn't. In fact, it can throw a whole paragraph out of kilter, as you can easily prove for yourself by trying to join any two sentences in the example on page 107 with *and* or any other conjunction. Or consider the disaster of joined Sally-cat sentences:

> Sally saw the cat, and it was a big cat, and it was a black cat; in other words, it was a big, black cat.

This is an extreme of simple-mindedness, of course, but at least it serves as a warning against thoughtless splices.

But, you may say, the Sally-cat sentences were hopeless from the start, and it is unfair to use them as examples. Is it? *Sally saw the cat* is a perfectly legitimate sentence—the very model, in fact, of the simple sentence: subject, verb, object. *John loves Mary. The garden needs rain. Lightning struck the tree. The car hit the lamp post.* These are all simple sentences. And they all can be made longer, more involved and interesting, including Sally's:

> Sally, caught by a sudden movement at the window, a movement so silent that she thought for a moment she

had seen the shadow of a passing bird, finally saw the big black cat.

That's only one of an almost limitless number of ways that the sentence could be changed from short to long. But it is enough to demonstrate two things: (1) to make a sentence longer you must provide additional material of some kind; and (2) the additional material should blend smoothly with the main part of the sentence, seeming a natural part of its growth. Note that the added material in the example above—"caught by a sudden movement, a movement so silent that . . ."—is firmly secured *inside* the sentence, hemmed in by *Sally* at one end and *saw* at the other. Thus the sentence grows from within, and its skin stretches naturally and easily to accommodate its expanding middle.

This expansion from within creates an extremely solid sentence, an all-of-a-piece structure with no loose ends. But such sentences should be alternated with looser, less formally constructed sentences for the sake of variety. You can make a sentence longer simply by adding detail to it, *after* the basic statement:

> Sally saw the cat, immense, velvety black, regally indifferent to her presence, its unblinking green stare as remote and self-possessed as an emperor's.

Details that are properly handled will never seem like hastily contrived bits and pieces pinned to the end of a sentence simply to make it longer; they will seem like a natural extension, part of the whole growing process.

But enough of Sally and her cat; now that they have served the useful purpose of proving that no sentence is ever really hopeless, they can be treated as exorcised ghosts. Your own sentences will be much easier to work with, simply because they are your own—and because they will have behind them the strength and purpose of a central idea.

The Basic Statement

In view of the staggering variety of sentences you encounter in a day's reading, you might think that sentences could have a hundred or even a thousand different patterns. Actually, they have only two of major importance: (1) the "strung-along" sentence, and (2) the periodic sentence.

Every sentence in the English language will fit into one of

these categories or will be a combination of both.* And once you understand the two patterns, you can write any kind of sentence you like—whether one word or one hundred words long—without the slightest fear of going off the rails.

You can master these patterns easily (they are surprisingly simple, once you learn to recognize them) if you first get a grip on one important principle—the principle of the *basic statement.*

All the following are basic statements:

1. Bells rang.
2. Love is blind.
3. The cat scratched Sally.
4. John gave his mother flowers.
5. The teacher considered him a good student.

These are basic statements because you cannot remove one word from any of them without damaging or destroying the meaning. They are pure, distilled extract-of-sentence, containing everything they need to make a complete statement and absolutely nothing else.

Every English sentence contains a basic statement. It may stand alone as one short sentence (as in the examples above), or it may be buried inside a longer sentence. But it is always present, it is always complete, and it is irreducible. It's the thing you have left after you chop away everything in a sentence except its essential meaning. And it's the thing you build on when you want to make a sentence longer.

You cannot subtract from a basic statement; you can only add to it. And you can add to it in two major ways. Those two ways are represented in the strung-along sentence and the periodic sentence.

The Strung-Along Sentence

The strung-along sentence is simply the basic statement with a string of details added to it. The string can be as long or as short as you care to make it. The basic statement does not change:

1. Basic statement: Bells rang.
   Strung-along sentence: Bells rang, *filling the air with their clangor, startling pigeons into flight from every belfry, bringing people into the streets to hear the news.*

* You will find the "balanced sentence," which represents one of the most important combinations, treated in the next chapter as part of the study of parallel structure.

2. Basic statement: The teacher considered him a good
student.

Strung-along sentence: The teacher considered him a
good student, *steady if not inspired, willing if not eager,
responsive to instruction and conscientious about his
work.*

Any basic statement can be converted to a strung-along
sentence by the addition of detail. For another example, look
at the description of the cat on page 110.

$$S \overset{\downarrow}{\_} V \overset{\downarrow}{\_} O$$

The Periodic Sentence

This is the sentence in which additional details are added
inside the basic statement. That basic statement is a tight little
structure; it must be broken in two at some point and spread
apart to make room for added cargo. Details are dropped into
the space between the two parts:

1. Basic statement: Love is blind.

Periodic sentence: Love, *as everyone knows except those
who happen to be afflicted with it,* is blind.

2. Basic statement: John gave his mother flowers.

Periodic sentence: John, *the tough one, the sullen kid
who scoffed at any show of sentiment,* gave his mother
flowers.

Delay, of course, is the secret weapon of the periodic sentence. By holding off the final words of the basic statement
until the last possible moment, the sentence builds its own
small feeling of suspense. And the reader is carried along
almost irresistibly to the end, for exactly the same reason he is
carried along by a mystery story—because he wants to know
"how it comes out."

The periodic is the most artful of all sentences. Its structure
has a kind of natural elegance, an air of perfectly controlled
movement, of assured grace. Its structure is so distinctive, in
fact, that it is not wise to place too many pure periodic sentences too close together. Space them out with the looser,
strung-along variety and with small, tight sentences, for contrast. Otherwise they will call attention to themselves. But an
occasional periodic sentence can add richness and tension to
writing that may otherwise seem too loose and casual.

to make sents longer:
1) join sm sents w/ connect. wds
2) add more info (adj or adv)
3) never repeat ideas in diff wds

The Combinations

Once you have learned to recognize and use the two major sentence patterns, you can forget about adhering to them strictly. They have served to make you aware of the sentence as a thing made up of movable parts. And although strictly patterned sentences can have enormous variety, a good sentence need not adhere strictly to the pure strung-along or pure periodic model. Indeed, it is far more likely to combine elements of both.

Again the ear must rule—and the ear must be attuned to the sound of the full paragraph. A perfectly patterned sentence may have a splendid ring when it is considered alone, but it may not join smoothly with the other sentences around it. In that case, adjust it. Add to it, subtract from it, juggle it this way and that; if it ceases to be a pure example of one particular pattern, who cares? The important thing is that it should sound right in relation to the sentences on either side of it.

Suppose you are working with a short, simple sentence—a sentence reduced to the barest basic statement:

> John was angry.

That may sound exactly right inside your paragraph—just short enough and sharp enough to have the force you want. In that case, leave it alone. But perhaps that nagging inner ear tells you that it isn't quite right; it needs something. So you make it a shade more periodic:

> John was *suddenly, violently* angry.

Or you make it even more periodic:

> John, *usually the calmest of men,* was *suddenly, violently* angry.

Or you decide to add detail at the end:

> John, *usually the calmest of men,* was *suddenly, violently* angry, *so angry that he lost control completely.*

Now the sentence is both periodic and loose. You could shake it up still more by moving some of the detail up front:

Usually the calmest of men, John was *suddenly, violently* angry . . .

The whole point is to take advantage of the flexibility of sentences, changing the pattern constantly in order to avoid monotony. In case you have the mistaken notion that a sentence is flexible only if it has a high emotional charge (John, certainly, was in a state before we got through with him), observe a calmer sentence in the process of change:

> Basic statement: Too many students work only for grades.
> Periodic sentence: Too many students, *obsessed with the idea that education is a contest,* work only for grades.
> Periodic and loose combined: Too many students, *obsessed with the idea that education is a contest,* work only for grades, *forgetting—or never realizing—that learning is not a race to be won but an adventure to be enjoyed.*
>
> or
>
> *Obsessed with the idea that education is a contest,* too many students work only for grades . . .

In short, any sentence that goes beyond basic statement is a thing of movable parts, regardless of content. So move the parts. Combine and recombine, shift and change, add and subtract. Shuffle the parts around until you have exactly the shade of emphasis you want. Experiment. Nobody can tell you in advance exactly how to order the parts; too much depends upon the sound of the sentence in relation to those around it.

Listen to your sentences. Consult your inner ear. Ask yourself constantly: Does this sound right? Does it blend smoothly and logically with the sentences around it? Does it vary enough in structure to avoid monotony? If it doesn't, move in. Start shoving those words and phrases around until that inner ear approves.

Selecting the Details

Most students grasp easily the technique of adding details to a sentence. What stumps them is the job of actually making up the details. They know *how* to add but not *what* to add. Faced with the necessity of filling out with detail a sentence they have already labored long to produce, they respond with a gloomy and hopeless, "I can't think of another thing."

If you count yourself among this despairing crew, it's time you realized that every time you say you "can't think of another thing" you are talking nonsense. Think "house." Your mind swarms with rooflines, windows, rooms, furniture, colors, noises, smells, seasons, streets, lawns, plaster, plumbing, porches, pets, and people. Think "ran." Instantaneously your mind re-creates the sound of pounding feet and straining breath, the feel of the wind on your face or the stitch in your side, the sense of panic or pleasure that accompanied the running. Think "dog," think "book," think "popularity," think anything you like. You will always think of other things as well. The truth is that you can't *not* think of other things; it is humanly impossible.

Your own mind—every human being's mind—is a giant memory bank storing bits and pieces of everything you have experienced, everything you have ever seen or touched or tasted or smelled or heard or thought or felt. Certainly you have forgotten a great many things, but the wealth of detail remaining is inexhaustible. Short of cutting off your head, you couldn't get rid of it even if you wanted to. So don't worry about being in short supply when it comes to details. You have your own private bank, overflowing with them. All you need is a key to the vaults.

Any word in any basic statement can be the key (excepting only words like "the" and "a" and "but" and "yet," which have no counterpart in real life). Suppose that you must add detail to this sentence:

The class read the assignment.

Immediately you have three words that have literally hundreds of associations in your mind: *class, read, assignment* (subject, verb, object of verb). Any one of them, or all of them, can be enriched and extended.

Not all sentences, of course, have this simple subject-verb-object structure, for not every verb takes a direct object. For your purposes, that doesn't matter. You need not know the precise grammatical terms for all the elements in a sentence in order to work with those elements. The important thing to remember is that the subject, the verb, and *anything that follows the verb* can be expanded.

Start with the subject.

Expanding the Subject

The easiest way to start the details flowing is to think of the subject as being followed by a pause. Make yourself hear that pause. It is exactly the same kind of pause that occurs in your own conversation every day, in sentences like this:

> That boy, the one wearing glasses, is in my history class.
> My mother, after all this time, says I can't go.
> This piecrust, tough as it is, tastes pretty good.

Boy and *mother* and *piecrust* hang in the air, waiting for something more to be said about them. Exactly the same principle applies to a written sentence: *The class* (pause) *read the assignment.* If you make yourself hear that pause, it will drive you to say something more about the class.

To prime the pump, ask yourself questions about the class: What kind of class is it? What is its attitude? How does it behave? Where does it meet? What is the most outstanding thing about it? What word or words would you use to describe it? You can't answer all these questions in the pause after the word "class," of course, but you can pick out the answer that is most relevant, perhaps one of these:

1. The class, *a mixture of juniors and seniors in advanced math,* . . .

2. The class, *usually noisy and inattentive,* . . .

3. The class, *alarmed by the prospect of an early test,* . . .

4. The class, *apathetic at best but frozen now into attitudes of complete boredom,* . . .

5. The class, *with a subdued rustle of books and papers,* . . .

6. The class, *settling easily into its new quarters in the annex,* . . .

7. The class, *after trying unsuccessfully to divert Mr. Dunwiddy into a discussion of the football game,* . . .

For the sake of variety, the additions should occasionally appear ahead of the subject:

> *With a subdued rustle of books and papers,* the class . .
> *After trying unsuccessfully to divert Mr. Dunwiddy into a discussion of the football game,* the class . . .

The ear rules, as usual. Whether you put the new material

in front of the subject or behind it depends entirely upon your personal preference.

As a rule, picture-and-sound-effect details, or details that suggest feeling (*alarmed by the prospect*), are the most effective. On this basis, #1 above is the weakest: "The class, *a mixture of juniors and seniors . . .*" That's straight fact, conveying neither picture nor sound and without a hint of atmosphere. This sort of substitute subject is called an *appositive*. It means the same thing as *class;* you could drop *class* and write, "The mixture of juniors and seniors read the assignment." The appositive is a convenient and straightforward method of identification that you will use often, but you can nearly always improve it by adding an adjective to suggest an additional shade of meaning: *a lethargic mixture, a lively mixture, an uneasy mixture.*

Graphic details are more interesting than plain appositives —and more fun to write. Three ways to make details graphic are shown in the examples on page 116. You can use an adjective (*noisy, inattentive, apathetic*), a prepositional phrase (*with a subdued rustle*), or a verb form (*alarmed, frozen, settling, trying*). The ones using a verb form are usually the most effective, simply because they carry a hint of action. Verbs are so powerful that even in a subordinate position like this, held down to half their strength, they carry a big jolt of energy.

But don't stick to any one method of adding to your subject. Switch from one to the other. Combine them. Notice that all three work together in #4—the adjective and the verb form are combined with prepositional phrases:

> The class, *apathetic at best but frozen now into attitudes of complete boredom,* . . .

The possibilities for combination are practically limitless. You could even combine a straight appositive with the other elements in the example above, if you felt like it.

You may have noticed that each example on page 116 employs a slightly different principle in its presentation of detail. At the end of this chapter you will find exercises based on these examples; they will familiarize you quickly with the various methods.

Expanding the Verb

You can expand the verb by showing how its action progresses:

> The class read, *listlessly at first, and then with growing interest,* the *day's* assignment.

Notice that *day's* has been slipped in ahead of *assignment.* Somehow *assignment* all by itself seemed bare and inadequate; the rhythm demanded the extra word (read the sentence over aloud to see whether you agree). An additional phrase describing the assignment would probably be better yet. Somehow, added weight in a verb section demands more weight at some other point.

Any phrase that tells how or when a verb acts is, of course, related grammatically to the verb, not to the subject or the object. But it's often easier to think of a how-or-when phrase while you are working with the subject, as in #7:

> The class, *after trying unsuccessfully to divert Mr. Dunwiddy into a discussion of the football game,* read the assignment.

Obviously, it's the reading and not the class that came "after." But the example is included under methods of adding detail to the subject rather than the verb simply because you are most likely to think of it at that point. And certainly it sounds better after *class* than it would sound after *read.* (Try reading it aloud both ways if you doubt this.)

Or you could even add the phrase after the object:

> The class read the assignment, *after trying unsuccessfully . . .*

You needn't worry about the grammatical distinctions. Just look at your verb, ask yourself how you can add to it by describing how or when it happened, and let the new material fall where it makes sense and sounds right. The grammar will take care of itself.

Expanding the Rest of the Sentence

The simplest way to expand the rest of the sentence is to look for its most important noun (often this will be a direct object) and follow it with an appositive—a word or phrase that means the same thing: "I saw Mr. Hassenfeffer, *the manager.*" "The class read the assignment, *a full chapter.*" The appositive, of course, simply provides additional identification for the word preceding it, making it more specific.

Sometimes a simple appositive is all you need (depending, as usual, upon the demand of your ear for rhythm). But often you will want to add more than that, and you can give your sentence more interest by adding details to the appositive. For example:

1. I saw Mr. Hassenfeffer, *the manager, a huge man with a flattened nose and beady eyes.*
2. The class read the assignment, *a full chapter, with a dismaying number of difficult-looking statistical tables.*
3. I saw Mr. Hassenfeffer, *the manager, flat-nosed, beady-eyed, on guard every minute.*
4. The class read the assignment, *a full chapter, dull, difficult, statistic-packed.*
5. I saw Mr. Hassenfeffer, *the manager, who gave me one alert, suspicious glance and then ignored me.*
6. The class read the assignment, *a full chapter so crowded with statistics that most of the students were ready to give up in despair before the end of the period.*
7. I saw Mr. Hassenfeffer, *the manager, waving his arms like a madman and turning slowly purple.*
8. The class read the assignment, *a full chapter covering trade relations before the war and illustrated with statistical tables.*

Notice the heavy use of prepositional phrases in all the additions in these examples: *with a flattened nose . . . , with a dismaying number, of . . . statistical tables, on guard,* etc. This is characteristic. In fact, one way to help yourself think of additional details is to add a preposition that forces you to ask a question: "I saw Mr. Hassenfeffer, *the manager, a huge man with . . .*" With what? your mind asks, and you are driven to answer: *with red whiskers, with a bulging briefcase, with a reputation for scaring the wits out of new employees. With* is usually the best one to start the details rolling. Others follow: *a full chapter with* (with what?) *. . . with a dismaying number of* (of what?) *. . . of statistical tables on* (on what?) *. . . on trade relations*—and so forth, almost endlessly.

It is a mistake, however, to stick only to prepositional phrases when you expand an object (or any other noun that comes after the verb). Notice that the sentences in #5–8 contain verb forms of various sorts. In #7–8 they go straight from the noun (*manager, chapter*) into a verb form (*waving, covering*). Semi-verbs like this are called *participles.* They have enough verb energy to add life to a descriptive passage.

You can also, of course, convert prepositional phrases into adjectives, as in #3: *flat-nosed, beady-eyed* instead of *with a flattened nose and beady eyes.* It's a good idea to telescope a prepositional phrase into one descriptive word whenever possible; and placing the descriptive word or words after the noun instead of ahead of it adds considerable zest because it upsets the usual word pattern. *The manager, flat-nosed, beady-eyed* sounds, for some reason, much more sinister than *The flat-nosed, beady-eyed manager.* The point here is not to use one word pattern to the exclusion of another but to vary them constantly, remembering that an unusual pattern is likely to give special emphasis.

Summary

Written sentences should have the sound of speech—intelligent, highly ordered speech that sounds completely natural to the listening inner ear of the reader. The means to this naturalness is through variety in sentence patterns: basic statements, strung-along sentences, periodic sentences, combinations. By learning to add detail in various ways to a basic statement, you can create any of these patterns; and by alternating them, by striving consciously for variety, by listening to your sentences as well as looking at them, you can create the natural cadence of the human voice.

The big obstacle that most student writers must overcome is the conviction that any sentence, once written, is an immovable and unchangeable object, like a chunk of concrete or an engraving on steel.

> *You must remember that a sentence is a thing of movable parts, an endlessly adaptable structure that is completely subject to the writer's will, shrinking or expanding to fit the sound and sense he chooses to give it.*

So relax. Loosen up. Play boldly with sentences. Combine, convert, shift, change, add, subtract, divide, multiply. Take chances. The more you experiment, the more you will learn.

to prod rhythm writing (1) vary sent length short 5 y med 6 y long 10 y (2) vary sent struct

QUESTIONS

1. Why is a child likely to believe that written sentences have nothing to do with spoken language?
2. In what sense is reading "almost as much an act of hearing as of seeing"?
3. Written sentences should sound like natural speech but cannot actually be natural speech. Explain.
4. What is the first principle of rhythm in writing?
5. What is a basic statement?
6. Describe the difference between a strung-along sentence and a periodic sentence.
7. What are the three main places in a sentence where details can be added?
8. Name three ways of constructing graphic details, illustrating each method with an example not taken from the text.
9. How do you add details to a verb?
10. What is an appositive? Give an example. How can a preposition help you to think of details to add to an appositive?

ASSIGNMENT

1. Reduce all the following sentences to basic statements:

   a. Looking from the mountain road above like a small tumble of children's toys left carelessly behind on the desert floor, the village slept in the sun, its streets empty, its houses shuttered and silent.

   b. The old man ate noisily, making a great clatter with his silverware, blowing on his coffee, smacking his lips with pleasure.

   c. Whatever else he may have been, however rude or quarrelsome or untidy, he was honest in all his dealings in every way.

   d. As he left the town behind he gained speed, pushing the little car faster and faster through the flat countryside that stretched endlessly to right and left of a highway as smooth and flat as the blade of a knife.

   e. The telephone rang, its shrill summons bringing everybody in the room to frightened attention.

2. Write a strung-along sentence *at least twenty words long* using each of the basic statements below as a starting point. Do not change the basic statement; just add to it. (See examples, pages 111–112.)

   a. The moon rose.
   b. The man was dead.

    c. He longed to be free.
    d. She liked the song.
    e. They had a good time.

3. Using each of the basic statements below, write five periodic sentences *at least fifteen words long*. (See examples, page 112.)

    a. Mary left the room.
    b. The world's greatest invention is the safety pin.
    c. Hate is based on fear.
    d. The man was dead.
    e. The circus was his life.

4. Select five of the ten sentences you have just written and add details that will make each one a combination of strung-along and periodic.
5. Expand the subject of the sentence below in the seven different ways illustrated on page 116 (#1–7). Follow the patterns exactly.

    The old man shuffled out of sight.

6. Expand the verb of each of the following sentences.

    a. The girl walked across the playground.
    b. The boy talked about fishing.

7. Add a simple appositive to the noun at the end of each sentence below:

    a. He liked the car.
    b. John read the book.
    c. They listened to the lecture.
    d. It was a special chair.
    e. He called the dog.

8. Using both prepositional phrases and participles, add detail to each of the appositives in the five sentences you have just written. Make each sentence *at least fifteen words long*.
9. Add an appositive and a *who* clause to the sentence below, following the pattern shown in #5, page 119.

    They asked for Mrs. Smith.

10. Write a sentence containing an appositive and a *so . . . that* comparison as shown in #6, page 119.

VOCABULARY

1. Define each of the following words:

adhering	exorcised	paradox
arbitrarily	implication	repetitive
erratic	inexhaustible	subconscious
	irreducible	

2. Below are the first few words of six incomplete sentences. Finish each of the sentences, using all of the following: (1) the word shown in parentheses with each; (2) an appositive; and (3) at least one prepositional phrase. The three items need not be used in the order given here, but all three must appear in each sentence.

   a. Although John had worked out a . . .   (*adhering*)
   b. He managed to . . .   (arbitrarily)
   c. The rhythm of . . .   (erratic)
   d. The ghosts . . .   (exorcised)
   e. We can only guess at . . .   (implication)
   f. The resources of . . .   (inexhaustible)

3. Follow each of the statements below with a second statement that explains the first in different words.

   a. A basic statement is irreducible;
   b. Writing that sounds natural is a paradox;
   c. The speaker was needlessly repetitive;
   d. His fear was subconscious;

10

Parallel Structure

Parallel structure, fully understood and put to use, can bring about such a startling change in composition that student writers sometimes refer to it as "instant style." It can add new interest, new tone, new and unexpected grace to even the most pedestrian piece of writing.

Unfortunately, a great many students (particularly those who were frightened by a grammar book early in life and have never fully recovered) never master parallelism simply because they are scared off by the definition. It's a definition cast in grammatical terms because it deals with a grammatical structure. The grammar-shy student takes one look at it and falls into a faint, sure that he has met the evil eye itself.

The irony of this is that the definition of parallel structure is actually a good deal harder to understand than parallel structure itself. The sensible thing to do, therefore, is to ignore the definition for the time being and to learn parallel structure the way you learned to talk—by listening to it.

Look for the Common Denominator

Parallelisms range all the way from the very simple to the extremely complex, but they all have one thing in common. You should have little difficulty finding this common denominator in the following examples:

> 1. He was the kind of man who knew what he wanted, who intended to get it, and who allowed nothing to stand in his way.
> 2. He wanted to walk out, to get in his car and drive forever, to leave and never come back.
> 3. They went to London, to Paris, to Rome.
> 4. He felt that Mary had changed, that she had moved into another world, and that she had left him behind.
> 5. If we are to survive, if we are to have even the hope of surviving, we must end the nuclear race.
> 6. To know you are right is one thing; to prove it, quite another.

The common denominator, of course, is the repetition of some element in the sentence. It is *not*, you will notice, the repetition of an idea.

> *A parallelism does not say the same thing in different words. The repetition is a repetition of* structure.

Look at #1. In this, the *who* clause is repeated: the man *who knew, who intended, who allowed.* Each clause makes a separate point, but each has the same structure.

In #2, the infinitive (*to* plus verb) repeats itself: *to walk, to get, to leave.*

In #3, it's the prepositional phrase: *to London, to Paris, to Rome.*

In #4, it's the *that* clause (commonly called a noun clause):

that Mary had changed, that she had moved, that she had left.
Notice that the tense of the verb remains the same, although
the verb itself changes.

In #5, the repetition is an *if* clause. This is an economical
method, by the way, of setting up all the *if*'s in any kind of
proposition—rather a handy thing to have around if you are
working with an "iffy" sort of thesis, particularly as you sum
up an argument: "If, then, such-and-such is true, if so-and-so
is right, if the situation is thus, then . . ." The repeated structure lends grace to logic, and the sentence resolves itself into
a triumphant final flourish.

The last one, #6, is an example of a "balanced sentence."
The infinitives *to know* and *to prove* are parallel, and the two
clauses are balanced on either side of a semicolon. Since both
clauses deal with the same idea (rightness), it is not necessary
to repeat the first clause in its entirety. In fact, the abruptness
of the second clause adds emphasis.

Balance, of course, is always inherent in parallelism. Various parts of the sentence balance themselves against each
other, weight for weight. Phrase balances with phrase, clause
with clause, idea with idea, thus creating a strong and satisfying sense of interior wholeness in a sentence.

The foregoing examples represent only a fraction of the
parallels possible with the English language. The more you
practice, the more ways you will discover. You can, for example, use a doubtful parallel:

> If we are to survive, if we are to have even the hope of
> surviving, we must end the nuclear race, and we must end
> it soon.

Or you can place whole sentences in parallel position, even
whole paragraphs. You can use parallels within parallels, in
patterns of increasing intricacy. The main thing is to begin.

ASSIGNMENT

1. Complete the unfinished sentence below with a series of
   who clauses:

   He always made trouble. He was the kind of boy who . . .

2. Complete with a series of infinitive phrases, using a different infinitive for each phrase:

   To be popular, she thought, she needed only to . . .

3. Using *to* as your preposition, complete this sentence with a series of prepositional phrases:

   In desperate search for a cure, he went to . . .

4. Using *of* as your preposition, complete this sentence with a series of prepositional phrases:

   She was afraid of everything, of . . .

5. Complete this with a series of *that* clauses:

   He complained that the children made too much noise, that . . .

6. Write a sentence beginning with three *if* clauses.
7. Write a sentence ending with three *if* clauses.
8. Complete the sentence below by *interrupting* it with two parallel *if* clauses:

   The problem of race relations, if . . . , and if . . . , must be solved.

9. Write a balanced sentence modeled on #6 on page 124 but using different infinitives.
10. Write a sentence that contains a double parallel.

The Smaller Parallels

The parallels you have studied so far have been stylistic, or literary, and therefore relatively sophisticated. In effect, you have started your study of parallels at the top, on the theory that this provides the best possible vantage point for watching operations at ground level—the small, simple parallels used every day in all kinds of writing.

These smaller parallels are exceedingly important, for any big, swooping parallel—like a bridge—needs solid support on the ground.

> *Whenever a sentence contains two or more similar elements, these elements must be kept parallel, no matter how small they are.*

In a series of nouns, for example, each item must be a noun. In a series of adjectives, each item must be an adjective; and so forth:

Nouns:

> *Not:* She liked ball games, hootenannies, hikes, and going to picnics.
> *But:* She liked ball games, hootenanies, hikes, and *picnics.*

That "going to" in the first example throws the whole parallel out of kilter. It's the kind of awkwardness that hits a reader's ear like the squawk of an unoiled hinge. Watch out for similar jarring notes in the following:

Adjectives:

> *Not:* He was lazy, good-humored, likeable, and sort of a crook.
> *But:* He was lazy, good-humored, likeable, and *slightly crooked.*

Adverbs:

> *Not:* She walked steadily and in a big hurry.
> *But:* She walked steadily and *swiftly.*

Verbs:

> *Not:* She combed her hair, powdered her nose, and her lipstick was checked.
> *But:* She combed her hair, powdered her nose, and *checked her lipstick.*

Suppose you are one of those students so impervious to grammar that you can't tell an adverb from an aardvark. You can still keep your parallels lined up. Use your ear and your common sense. You can tell whether words need to be alike or not. Take it from there.

The same principle operates in relation to pairs. Pairs are usually balanced on either side of *and, but,* and *or.* Keep them equal, as shown in the corrections below:

> He was an expert driver and could also repair cars. (driver and *mechanic*)
> He was intelligent but a boring boy.   (intelligent but *boring;* or, *a brain* but *a bore*)
> Her ambition was to act in movies and playing certain roles.   (to act in movies and *to play* . . .)
> She wanted either money or to be famous.   (money or *fame*)

It's always a good idea to take a sharp look at what you use with *and, but,* and *as well as,* particularly at the tail end of a sentence. That's where the slippage is likely to occur:

> The trip into town had been both difficult and a great expense.   (both difficult and *expensive*)
>
> He wanted to pour all his effort into the job, to do it well, but keeping the time down as much as possible. (but *to do it quickly*)
>
> She worked hard to maintain her high grades, but she yearned for popularity as well as being recognized as a good student.   (for popularity as well as *academic success*)

Some of the trickiest parallels to control are those using *either/or, neither/nor, not only/but also,* and *first/second/third.* The first two pairs, particularly, are tricky:

> *Not:* Either I'm always in debt or in trouble.
> *But:* Either I'm always in debt or I'm always in trouble,
>
> or
>
> I'm always either in debt or in trouble.
>
> *Not:* She is the kind of woman who will neither change her mind nor her hair style.
> *But:* She is the kind of woman who will change neither her mind nor her hair style.

The easiest way to check these two for proper position is to call a halt, mentally, immediately after *either* or *neither* and check the weight on both sides of *or* or *nor:*

> I'm always either   in debt   or   in trouble.
> She could be neither   kind   nor   cruel.

The weight must be the same on both sides. Word balances word, phrase balances phrase. The same principle governs *not only/but also:*

> That will scare not only   Sally   but also   the cat.
> They hoped to go not only   to London   but also   to Paris.

The problem with *first/second/third* is that one item can easily slip out of line: "First, the photography is poor; second, the sound track is below average; third, I don't think it's in very good taste." That last item is, of course, out of parallel; write "third, the whole thing is in poor taste," and it falls into line.

The first item in any series sets the pattern, and all other items must comform to it. The first item in the following example is a *that* clause; therefore, *that* must be repeated after *second* and *third*:

> After he entered college he realized clearly, first, that he should have worked harder in high school; second, that he would have to work hard now to keep up; and third, that he could succeed only by learning self-discipline.

Compare this example with #4 on page 124. Structually they are exactly the same. The only difference is that here the clauses are numbered. The structure is brought to your attention again because you may get so involved with numbering that you forget about keeping the items parallel.

The smallest of all the parallels has been kept until last—the use of articles (*a, an, the*) and prepositions (*to, by, for, from,* etc.) in a series. The rule:

> *If you repeat an article or a preposition once, repeat it every time—or not at all.*

For example:

> A house, a yard, a garden, and a pool.
>
> or
>
> A house, yard, garden, and pool.
> For love, for honor, for fame, or for money.
>
> or
>
> For love, honor, fame, or money.

Summary

Some parallels are a matter of simple logic. Controlling them is mainly a housekeeping chore, a necessary straightening and tidying-up that every writer learns to do as a matter of course, as part of his job. The subtler and more complex parallels are the real challenge and the true delight of writing. Requiring the most artful balance of many elements, they are exciting things to handle; but even more exciting is the immediate and startling improvement they can make in your writing style.

Parallelism on any level is simply, in the final analysis, control. Keep all elements of equal value parallel, whether they are big elements or small, and your sentences can't straggle off raggedly this way and that. They will have the sense of wholeness and balance, of architectural soundness, that pleases the ear and satisfies the mind.

––––––––––––

QUESTIONS

1. What is the best way to learn parallel structure?
2. Parallelism "is a repetition of *structure*." Explain.
3. Give an example of a balanced sentence.

ASSIGNMENT

1. Each of the sentences below contains some kind of faulty parallelism. Rewrite each sentence correctly.

   a. She planned a trip to the country, a visit with her grand-mother, and taking long hikes with her cousin.
   b. The old man was gentle, kind, and gave away a lot of money to the poor.
   c. He put the model airplane together neatly, accurately, and with a great deal of skill.
   d. The boy wiped the windshield, cleaned off the dirty headlights, polished the chrome trim, and even the hub-caps were checked.
   e. She was a good cook and also kept house well.
   f. She was beautiful but a spoiled child.
   g. He hoped either to be elected president of his class or make the highest grades.
   h. He was intelligent as well as having a lot of friends.
   i. He had to have the suit both altered and to have it cleaned.
   j. The thing he most looked forward to was a hot meal and having a hot bath.
   k. He enjoyed going to the movies as well as trips to the theater.
   l. Either the boys disliked or ignored him.
   m. That girl will neither take advice from her parents nor her friends.
   n. Their purpose was not only to take special courses in science but in art.
   o. The committee is not only working hard to preserve historical landmarks but is also interested in developing a local museum.
   p. They believe that a museum will promote greater in-terest in local history, that it will enrich the lives of

school children in the community, and will become a major tourist attraction.

q. Many students believe that to be popular is happiness.

r. Study develops the mind; exercise develops the body; and understanding is developed by experience.

s. He made it clear, first, that he had no faith in the project; second, that he would not support it; and that, third, he would advise his friends against it.

t. They arrived in town by bus, by train, by plane, and even walking.

2. President John F. Kennedy's Inaugural Address contained a number of striking parallelisms. Find at least five in the selections from the Address, below. Copy them exactly.

We observe today not a victory of party but a celebration of freedom, symbolizing an end as well as a beginning, signifying renewal as well as change. . . .

. . . Let the word go forth from this time and place, to friend and foe alike, that the torch has been passed to a new generation of Americans, born in this century, tempered by war, disciplined by a hard and bitter peace, proud of our ancient heritage, and unwilling to witness or permit the slow undoing of those human rights to which this nation has always been committed, and to which we are committed today at home and around the world.

So let us begin anew, remembering on both sides that civility is not a sign of weakness, and sincerity is always subject to proof. Let us never negotiate out of fear, but let us never fear to negotiate.

Now the trumpet summons us again—not as a call to bear arms, though arms we need; not as a call to battle, though embattled we are; but a call to bear the burden of a long twilight struggle, year in and year out, "rejoicing in hope, patient in tribulation," a struggle against the common enemies of man: tyranny, poverty, disease and war itself.

And so, my fellow Americans, ask not what your country can do for you; ask what you can do for your country.

3. Below is a description of an animal lab. Choose a subject of your own—perhaps a library, a dormitory, a restaurant, any place you have observed closely—and write a description that imitates the passage below. Match its sentence structure, parallels, figures of speech, etc., with suitable constructions of your own.

The animal lab is full of strange, muted sounds. Somewhere down the hall, behind closed doors, monkeys gossip incessantly, their voices thin, bored, faintly exasperated, like the voices of empty-headed office girls on an endless coffee break. Now and then a lemur's cry—high, sweet, full of grief and hope—breaks through the monkeys' mindless chatter. And something else whispers in the air, a small rustling and scuttling sound, anciently familiar and vaguely disquieting: rats are nearby.

They are, in fact, nearby in great numbers, in the big colony room. These are elegant rats, refined rats, plump and docile and immaculate, white of fur and innocently pink of claw and tail. Science has bred out of them nearly every resemblance to their ugly ancestors. These placid aristocrats have never seen a ship's hold, or a garbage dump, or a littered alley; they have never run from snapping dogs nor crept at night through secret tunnels in the walls of decayed tenements. But they still make, in their clean wire cages, the ageless sound that rats in movement have always made.

4. Select a student from your class in composition (preferably a student you do *not* know well) and write a description of him (or her). Do this assignment during class, while you can actually observe your subject. Give enough concrete detail to make him recognizable, but do not give his name.

In addition to actual physical description, indicate also the kind of person you think your subject might be, guessing at his inner thoughts, his ambitions, his attitudes. This will take some imagination. Except for literal description, you will be treating your subject almost as a fictional character. Use third person only. And finally, *use at least one example of each kind of parallel structure shown in examples #1–6 on page 124.*

VOCABULARY

1. Define the following words:

disquieting	inherent
docile	intricacy
immaculate	pedestrian
impervious	vantage

2. Choose the word from the above list that most nearly fits the meaning of each sentence below:

a. The pattern in the lace was extremely delicate and complex, a web of leaves and flowers interwoven with gold thread.

b. An iron-willed man, he could not be reached by any appeal to his emotions.

    c. From the attic window they had a splendid view of everything that went on in the street.

    d. Every word, every gesture suggested a strong instinct for drama.

    e. She was quiet, submissive, and willing to learn.

    f. His writing style is quite ordinary.

    g. His white shirt was spotlessly clean.

    h. She refused to believe the rumor, but it made her uneasy.

3. Using all the words in the vocabulary list above, write four sentences, each containing one of the parallelisms illustrated in examples #1–6 on page 124.

11

A Way with Words

You have spent a great deal of time learning some rather difficult techniques of style. Now it behooves you to see to it that you have a vocabulary worthy of those techniques.

Don't expect to write well with a vocabulary limited to the perfectly familiar—and therefore perfectly easy—words you already know. It can't be done, and the sooner you face that hard fact the faster your progress will be. Other things being equal, the bigger your vocabulary, the better your writing. It's a matter of simple arithmetic. The more words you know, the more choices you can make; and the more choices you can make, the better chance you have of finding the exact word you need at any given time—what the French call *le mot juste*, the word that fits precisely the thought you want to express.

You have been working regularly with vocabulary assignments, but you should begin now, if you have not already done so, to intensify your efforts to improve and enlarge your word supply. Don't waste your time envying the lucky few who, through wide reading or constant association with unusually fluent people, already have large vocabularies. Yours can be just as large, or larger. Don't try to find excuses for a poor vocabulary (I'm too dumb, I'm too busy, I've got other things on my mind). A poor vocabulary can't be excused—not in this day and age. It can only be explained. And the explanation can be summed up in one word: laziness. If you want a good vocabulary, you can have it. But don't expect it to come to you without effort; you've got to go after it.

Go after it first in a big general way, by reading. Read for pleasure. Read everything you can find on any subject that interests you. Read short stories, novels, articles. Read the newspaper. Read matchbook covers. Read everything. Soak up words wherever you find them. The more you read, the more words you will know.

When you find a word you don't know, *look it up.* You've probably heard that so many times during your school career that it no longer registers. Make it register. LOOK IT UP. Take a fresh look at those words. They mean something. Get a pocket dictionary and park it in your hip pocket or your purse so that it's always handy, and *use* it. Underline new words and list them separately on your own private word list. Don't try to persuade yourself you'll remember it just because you looked it up. You won't. Write it down. Install an imaginary red light in your brain that says STOP—LOOK IT UP—LIST IT every time you see or hear an unfamiliar word.

As soon as you have a new word nailed down in your mind, use it in conversation. Make a game of it, not a classroom exercise. Try at least one new word a day, and pick an audience that you aren't afraid of—your little sister or your barber or even your dog. Get used to the new word in your mouth. You'll be surprised at how quickly it loses its strangeness. Tell your prattling little sister that she's *loquacious,* tell the barber you want an *orthodox* haircut, tell Rover he's entirely too *obstreperous.* In no time at all, the new words will have moved comfortably into position as part of your working vocabulary.

Then if your new words are met with surprise by your enemies, who sometimes have the annoying habit of dropping their jaws and saying "Wozzat mean? Whatcha talkin' about?" you can have the exquisite pleasure of replying, "Don't be *obtuse,* Charlie." It isn't wise to do this, of course, if you think Charlie might look up *obtuse,* particularly if he is bigger than you are and given to violence.

Synonyms and Antonyms

In addition to a dictionary, you need one other tool for improving your vocabulary: Roget's *Thesaurus.* You can get it in a paperback student edition for just about the price of an ice-cream soda; and it may prove to be the most valuable tool of all. The *Thesaurus* has two sections—an alphabetical index in the back, and a huge body of idea-centered groups of words, with their synonyms and antonyms. Look up a word for almost any idea you want to express and you will find not only all the other words that mean the same thing but also all sorts of related words and phrases, the kind that tease at the edges of your mind but that you can never quite pin down. You know what you want to say, but you can't quite say it? Look in Roget.

Roget's *Thesaurus* is not a dictionary. It gives no definitions. But you will almost invariably find exactly the word you want. A word may be followed by a dozen synonyms, or more, but suddenly you see one of them and think, "That's it." It locks instantly into place in your mind, wonderfully and exactly right, the very word you were looking for.

Here, for example, are just a few of the words Roget lists in connection with the single verb "inquire": *seek, look for, reconnoiter, explore, rummage, ransack, pry, peer, pursue, scrutinize, ferret out, unearth, agitate, investigate, analyze, anatomize, dissect, sift, winnow*. These, remember, are just a *few* of those listed in the entry. If you want to know the others, get a copy of Roget and inquire within.

One of the most satisfying things about the *Thesaurus* is that it often supplies a choice where you think no choice exists. You have no doubt had the experience of writing a paper in which one word crops up insistently again and again. It begins to sound repetitious and dull, and you know it, but no matter how you cudgel your brains you can't think of anything to put in its place. This is where Roget comes to the rescue. If the word has a substitute, the *Thesaurus* will have it. And even if no substitute exists, the *Thesaurus* will probably give you hints for rephrasing an idea or shifting an emphasis, thus neatly solving the problem by avoiding it.

Best of all, Roget makes you aware as never before of the tremendous selection of words available to express every shade of meaning, all of them clustered around one word for easy picking and so cross-referenced that if you can't find what you want in one place you are directed elsewhere. You may not always know the meaning of every word given, but that's what the dictionary is for.

If, for example, you want to describe Charlie, that obnoxious fellow, you have the happy opportunity to choose from *abhorrent, despicable, odious, abominable, repulsive, malicious, rancorous, churlish, surly, invidious, venomous, hostile*, or *repulsive*—and that's just a beginning. Pick a good one and check it out with the dictionary, just to be sure you have the exact shade of meaning you want. The dictionary not only points out subtle differences in meaning but often supplies examples that help still further in making close distinctions. You will want to do your best by Charlie.

Nearly every classroom has a king-size dictionary, and many English classrooms have Roget's *Thesaurus* or a similar book of synonyms. But these are for classroom use. You should have a small pocket edition of each that you can call your own. Put your name on them. Use them constantly. Guard them. The world is full of pocket-book snatchers. Snarl menacingly at borrowers. When you have finally finished your formal education, nothing—not even a crisp new diploma—will be a prouder badge of distinction than these two books, tattered, dog-eared, and completely worn out from use.

Big Words and Small

A good writing vocabulary needs to be big, but that does not mean that it should be made up exclusively of big words. Most particularly, it does not mean a vocabulary in which big words are substituted for perfectly adequate small words. The writer who, in the mistaken belief that he will sound more dignified, insists on using polysyllabic words like *accompanied* instead of *went with, informed* instead of *told,* merely succeeds in sounding like a stuffed shirt.

Generally speaking, when you can choose between an easy, familiar expression and one that seems more "dignified," the easier word is the better choice *if it means exactly the same thing.* The more formal expression may be used occasionally, simply for the sake of variety, but consistent formality will make your writing sound impossibly prim and genteel. Some of the high-flown substitutes that crop up all too often in bad writing are these:

accompany (go with)	manner (way)
appeared to be (seemed)	obtained (got)
consumed (ate)	possessed (had)
desired (wanted)	received (got)
implemented (followed up)	required (needed)
individual (he, she, man, woman, etc.)	securing (getting)
	similar to (like)
informed (told)	stated (said)

No hard and fast rule can be laid down against using any of these expressions, since you may on occasion use any one of them without ill effect. But give them as wide a berth as possible. The best way to guard yourself against them is to avoid the temptation of trying to *sound* dignified. Your writing will have natural dignity if it is a serious and thoughtful presentation of your ideas. The moment you try to doctor it up with high-flown, stately-sounding, polysyllabic substitutes for direct and simple words, you become the victim of creeping pomposity.

Always be suspicious of any impulse on your part to impress a reader with your dignity. No reader was ever warmed by a blast of hot air. The thing to look for, always, is *le mot juste*—not the pompous substitute-word that trumpets what a smart fellow you are, but the precisely chosen word that instantly transmits an exact shade of meaning.

But don't make the mistake of depending always upon the short or familiar words. Some are so familiar that they no longer have any specific meaning. This is particularly true of descriptive words like *good, nice, pretty, ugly, bad, awful, big, little, fast, slow, funny, crazy, great, fine*—and a host of others that you recognize instantly as the currency of everyday speech. They are appallingly inadequate in writing, and these words, above all others, should be traced through Roget and the dictionary until you find a more precise meaning for your particular purpose. Just to get an idea of the immense choice available, look at some of the possible substitutes available for the word "crazy":

> *insane, mad, lunatic, unhinged, unbalanced, psychopathic, cracked,* non compos mentis, *touched, bereft of reason, moonstruck, scatterbrained, maniacal, delirious, irrational, lightheaded, incoherent, rambling, doting, wandering, amuck, frantic, raving, pixilated, eccentric, demented, deranged, schizophrenic.*

Or examine the shades of bigness in these substitutes for "big":

> *bulky, huge, mountainous, enormous, massive, impressive, important, weighty, considerable, vast, immense, stupendous, mighty, monstrous, titanic, gigantic, colossal, gargantuan, voluminous, mammoth, corpulent, burly, portly, elephantine.*

With such a wealth of words to choose from, poverty of expression is inexcusable. If you dwell in the slums of language, if you refuse to claim your inheritance, you have no one to blame but yourself. English is the richest language in the world, and for over a hundred years men have worked lovingly and patiently to gather it together in dictionary and thesaurus, to explain it and classify it for your convenience, so that you can pick and choose exactly what you want from it for the rest of your life. It is all freely yours, for the taking.

You can be a prince or a pauper, depending upon how much of your inheritance you choose to claim.

It's up to you.

The Solemn Vapors

Almost every student comes down once in a while with a bad case of abstractionitis, or Solemn Vapors, a writer's disease brought on by the excessive use of big, general words like *equality, justice, patriotism, democracy, morality, idealism, happiness.* These are important and necessary words, and it would be impossible for us to get along without them, but they are a special hazard in writing because they tempt a writer into believing he has said something profound when he may have actually said almost nothing—at least nothing that a reader can take hold of in any real way.

An abstraction is any word that applies to a large class of things rather than to any single, concrete object or idea. Every word is in some measure an abstraction, but some abstractions are more general than others. *Structure,* for example, is more general than *house, house* is more general than *hovel,* and *hovel* is more general than *a miserable little shack with broken windows and a sagging door.* The more general the meaning of a word, the more abstract it is likely to be.

Too many abstract words make for vagueness, even meaninglessness. Good writing is specific; it makes things real. Observe that as you move away from abstraction toward something more specific—from *structure* to *miserable shack*—you create a sharper mental image and therefore a stronger sense of reality. You can never get away from abstractions entirely, but you should try constantly to pin them down, embody them in things that are real and tangible.

The opposite of abstract is *concrete.* Concrete words are words that stand for real things, things that appeal in one way or another to the senses. Unlike an abstraction, which exists only as a rather hazy mental concept, a concrete word is something you can see or hear or smell or taste or touch. And it is concrete words that give your writing color and texture and the solid feeling of realness.

Stick to concrete words as much as possible. If you are writing an essay on an abstract subject, pin it down quickly with specific examples that illustrate exactly what you mean. Don't float off on a cloud of vague and virtuous general terms.

Perhaps the best way to demonstrate the difference between concrete and abstract language is by a single example with which you are undoubtedly already familiar, a phrase that has become a classic example of the power in a concrete image as opposed to an abstraction. The phrase swept the country, instantly becoming a byword, simply because it translated an abstract idea into a vivid, immediately understood, specific image:

> Happiness is a warm puppy.

The abstractionist would have written:

> One characteristic of the condition of happiness is a quality of contentment or pleasure associated with complete physical comfort, satisfaction with a given environment, and a sense of being loved.

Even the most rigorous anti-sentimentalist would admit that the warm puppy says a great deal more than the abstraction.

Symptoms of the Solemn Vapors often include misty eyes, outthrust jaw, a tendency to clench the fists, and a warm feeling of self-righteousness in the area of the breastbone. If you feel an attack coming on, cold baths may help, but for best results go back to Chapter 6 for a quick review of the picture-frame paragraph. That should help you keep in touch with the things of this world.

Metaphor and Simile

The most effective way to make an abstraction concrete is by metaphor—a single vivid image that illustrates an idea. That warm puppy, for example, is a metaphor—an instantaneous representation of innocence, contentment, and love, a hundred times more vivid and meaningful than a dozen paragraphs of description or explanation.

> *A metaphor never explains; it creates an image, and the image explains itself.*

Oddly, the more vivid and apt a metaphor is, the more likely it is to turn into a cliché. Everybody likes it, and everybody uses it; and as a result it becomes so much a part of everyday speech that it loses all its original force and color. "Hitch your wagon to a star," for example, must have been a startlingly vivid figure of speech when it was first coined, but the picture has been rubbed out of it by universal use. As in "All that glitters is not gold" or "Birds of a feather flock together," the vividness has become triteness, and no self-respecting author uses such phrases except as brief allusions or after giving them playful new twists: "All that gold was not just glitter," "Birds of a very different feather," "An actress whose stardom is hitched to a wagon train."

The same kind of wear and tear affects similes. (A simile is a slowed-down metaphor; instead of jumping straight to its image it arrives by way of an "as" or "as if" or "like." Typical worn-out similes are *hungry as a bear, quick as a wink, old as the hills, feel like a million.* Avoid these expressions entirely in writing unless you can give them fresh appeal.

It is one of the ironies of writing that a good metaphor becomes a commonplace precisely because it expresses an idea so well, but the writer, whose whole purpose is to say things well, can't use commonplaces. His job is to seek always for new images, new metaphors that will translate ideas into pictures. For this he must fall back on his own experience and imagination. He must learn (and this is the whole secret of metaphor) to describe one thing by comparing it directly or indirectly to another:

> She pushed herself down the street slowly, patiently, like an indomitable old turtle, her immense body balanced precariously on stumpy legs, her small head retracted into the folds of her collar, only the humorous, curved beak of her nose protruding into the bitter air. The buckles of her flapping galoshes made a sound like the clatter of ancient claws.

Note that this metaphor is extended; each detail of the old woman's appearance relates one way or another to the turtle image—*immense body, stumpy legs, small head, retracted, curved beak, ancient claws.* In an extended metaphor, details must be kept consistent with the original image.

It is not necessary, however, to extend a metaphor to this length. One sentence can provide a single image before you move on to fulfill some other purpose in a paragraph. Note, in the examples below, how the metaphor or the simile is sometimes carried by a verb, sometimes by a noun or an adjective, sometimes by a combination of elements:

> . . . eyes as hard and wise and wary as an old turtle's
> . . . a jungle of ropes and pulleys and discarded scenery
> . . . her voice cut through his thoughts like a rusty file
> . . . a pasted-on smile
> . . . sausage-fingered
> . . . the craggy landscape of his face
> . . . music pulling at her feet

The principle for both metaphor and simile is the same: both of them make or imply a comparison between two things; one of the two things compared is literal, the other figurative.

A purely literal comparison—"She looks like her mother"—is not metaphorical. She quite literally does look like her mother. But "She looks like a thundercloud" is metaphorical. Nobody really looks like a thundercloud. The connotation, however, is clear. The lady is not feeling tranquil.

It is possible, of course, to use too many metaphors and similes in your writing. When this happens, the writing lacks some necessary hard edge of reality—it "goes soft." Nobody can tell you how much metaphor is too much, but you should be suspicious of your writing if it takes on a consistently dreamy, hazy quality that sounds pretty but never makes its point sharply and directly. Fortunately, the cure is not difficult. You need only train yourself to alternate metaphorical expression with abrupt, unadorned, precise statement. If you are naturally adept at metaphor, you probably have an ear that is naturally well tuned to language, and you will quickly appreciate the improvement in your style when you make it a little harder and more vigorous.

Most students, however, use far too little figurative language. You should experiment with it often, for it can give your writing greater excitement, a more interesting texture. Metaphors are usually more subtle than similes, and frequently more brilliant, but here again variety is the key. Use both—and every variety of both. It would probably be wise to hold similes down to one per paragraph: "like" and "as" and "as if" have a way of sticking out too obviously when they become too numerous. But let yourself go with all other kinds of metaphor. A good paragraph can probably support as many of them as you can dream up.

Allusion

Allusion is indirect reference, and it is simply another way to strike a responsive chord in a reader. Familiar allusions are easiest: "They were the Beatles of Westport High," "He has a Madison Avenue mentality," "He was the local Scrooge," "the neighborhood Dempsey," "the campus Claghorn."

Never explain an allusion. If the reader understands it, fine. He will be pleased at this sudden and unexpected thrust of the familiar into the line he is reading. If he doesn't understand it, no harm done. The meaning will usually be perfectly clear.

Allusions can range from the familiar to the highly literary, with stops in between for commonly recognized literary forms like children's verse and stories: "He was able to stay on this Jack Sprat diet only one week," "He could play fairly well, but he was no Pied Piper," "He had no taste for the role of cat looking at king." Any familiar literary reference can be used allusively, either seriously or ironically: "This brave new world requires brave new people," "I was not yet one-and-twenty, but I was full of rue," "He sat at the door like Cerberus," "Having accomplished nothing, they folded their tents and stole sheepishly away," "How do I hate algebra? Let me count the ways."

The wider your knowledge of literature, the richer your sources of allusion. Literary allusions are a particular source of pleasure for the discriminating reader, for they notify him in the subtlest possible way that the writer shares with him a common literary heritage. Unlike direct, factual quotations that require extra typographical details, the allusion is deftly woven into context, and from there it sends its secret signal to any reader equipped to receive it.

Summary

Increase your vocabulary consciously by reading, by using your thesaurus and your dictionary, by practicing new words in speech and writing until they become a natural and familiar part of your thinking process. To enrich your vocabulary is to enrich not only your writing but your life, for the more words you know the better you can understand and interpret your own experience.

Make abstractions real by using your senses. Translate big, vague terms into the tangible objects of real life. Make yourself *see* what you write about: give your ideas substance with specific details, with real things that have color and shape, things that can be touched or tasted or smelled or heard. Strive always toward realness.

For this realness use metaphor and simile. *Show* what you mean, in images. And use allusion to maintain the sense of friendly communication, of shared experience, with your reader. Connect, relate, compare—and thus delight.

QUESTIONS

1. What is *le mot juste?*
2. What should you do every time you come across a word that is new to you?
3. What is a synonym?
4. What is an antonym?
5. Describe Roget's *Thesaurus*. What was the original meaning of the word "thesaurus"?
6. Will your writing have more dignity if you make a point of using big words in place of smaller, more familiar words? Explain your answer.
7. Explain the meaning of this statement about vocabulary: "You can be a prince or a pauper, depending upon how much of your inheritance you choose to claim."
8. What does the author mean by the phrase, "the slums of language"?
9. What are the "Solemn Vapors"?
10. What is the difference between an abstract word and a concrete word? Give at least two examples (not the same ones used in the text).
11. What is the difference between a metaphor and a simile? Give examples.
12. What is an allusion?

ASSIGNMENT

1. Write a brief essay defending the idea that a student's personal copies of a pocket dictionary and a *Thesaurus*, worn out from use, may be better evidence of a good education than a diploma.
2. Look up the word "nice" in the dictionary. You may be surprised to learn its precise meaning, as opposed to the meaning it has for most people in ordinary conversation. Write a brief essay in which you do the following:
   a. Give the precise definition.
   b. Poke fun at the overuse of "nice," giving examples of its overuse.
   c. End your essay with a sentence that uses the word "nice" correctly.
3. Rewrite each of the following sentences so that it expresses the same idea in concrete rather than abstract terms. (For example, "Vigorous physical exercise before breakfast is an excellent way to start the day" can be made concrete by

saying "A few push-ups before breakfast can start the day right.")

   a. She was tired of domestic chores.
   b. The available reading material was very scanty.
   c. Certain physical characteristics gave evidence of his anger.
   d. Real elegance, to her, was jewelry.
   e. The daily consumption of some kind of fresh fruit is helpful in reducing the need for medical attention.
   f. He longed for contact with nature.
   g. His clothing was obviously old and worn.
   h. He was tired of the pressures of city life.
   i. He would have given a great deal for some kind of solid nourishment.
   j. What he needs is some kind of strong disciplinary treatment.

4. Choose one of the sentences below as the first sentence of a descriptive paragraph. Use an extended metaphor to complete the description. (See example on page 140.) Be sure to keep details consistent.

   a. She was as cool and graceful as a very elegant cat.
   b. He looked like a crafty intelligent old goat.
   c. She moved about the house like a fat, dignified hen.
   d. She was small and mouselike.

5. Write five sentences in which you make some kind of familiar allusion. (See examples on pages 141–142.) Be as original as possible.

6. Write five sentences in which you make a literary allusion. Your literature textbook may be helpful. Find a well-known quotation and work it into some meaning of your own. (See examples on page 142.)

VOCABULARY

1. Below is a list of words that are constantly overused. For *each* of the words, supply a list of at least ten other words that might be used in its place:

good	terrible	pretty
bad	wonderful	ugly
big	happy	dull
little	sad	exciting

2. Use *each* of the words below in a periodic sentence that contains at least fifteen words:

behooves	invidious	obtuse
corpulent	loquacious	odious
demented	malicious	orthodox
eccentric*	maniacal*	surly
gargantuan	obstreperous	

12
Odds and Ends and Means

A multitude of small sins against style can plague writing. They are mostly sins of carelessness. Taken singly they may not seem to amount to much, but several of them added together can spoil a writer's whole effect. So, just as any well-groomed person gives himself a final check before appearing in public, you should take care of certain stylistic details before letting any piece of writing go out of your hands.

Some of these sins of carelessness are minor, like a loose button or a crooked seam; others are as appalling as a grimy neck on a girl in a ball gown. Collected for your examination on the following pages are thirty of the most common ones. It is not really possible to classify all thirty in any kind of ascending (or descending) order according to offensiveness, but at least three deserve to be at the head of the list. The others are listed alphabetically for easy reference, but the Terrible Three come first. If you take any pride at all in your brainchild, you will not let it face the world until you have scrubbed out these abominations.

The Terrible Three

1. The *-wise* suffix: Some day the barbarian who started the fashion of adding *-wise* to the end of words will be identified, run to earth, and suitably punished—preferably by being forced to spend the rest of his life reading the compositions written by students who have followed in his footsteps. That would probably be best, justice-wise. . . .

The use of *-wise* as a suffix has become so prevalent that no word in the language seems to be safe from it. In the course

* Take special care to pronounce these two correctly.

of an average day you are likely to hear that the cafeteria is serving some great desserts pie-wise, that a girl is attractive clothes-wise, hair-wise, or face-wise, or that the weekend ahead looks pretty busy, study-wise.

It's enough to drive you crazy, style-wise.

Fortunately, the constant use of *-wise* is rapidly becoming a kind of national joke, generally recognized as an expression reserved for the hopelessly square. In a few years it may be laughed out of existence. But it's a good idea to avoid it like poison, meantime-wise.

2. The *type* and *type of* habit: Throw these out along with *-wise*. It is particularly barbarous to use *type* as an adjective: *I have the type father who loses his temper*. Even with an "of" added (*I have the type of father who . . .*) the expression is an assault on the ear of a discriminating reader.

Its use is bad partly because its meaning is nearly always subtly askew (usually the writer means *sort* or *kind* rather than *type*), but it is objectionable primarily because it has been overused to the point of nausea. Like *-wise* it has become the hallmark of the amateur, the inarticulate, the square. You can always change it for the better—usually by omitting it altogether. If you can't quite omit some needed shade of qualification that you think it adds, try one of the changes suggested below:

> *Not:* I have the type of father who loses his temper.
> *But:* I have a father who loses his temper.
>
> or
>
> My father has a quick temper.
>
> *Not:* She wasn't that type of girl.
> *But:* She wasn't that kind of girl.
>
> *Not:* She wore a Spanish-type costume.
> *But:* She wore a Spanish costume.
>
> or
>
> Her costume had a Spanish look.
>
> *Not:* He was a Charles Chaplin-type actor.
> *But:* His acting was Chaplinesque.
>
> or
>
> Like Charles Chaplin, he . . .
>
> *Not:* He used Hitler-type methods.
> *But:* He used Hitlerian methods.
>
> or
>
> He used Hitler-like methods.
>
> *Not:* Guerrilla-type warfare.
> *But:* Guerrilla warfare.

3. *Manner* and *nature* phrases: *Manner* and *nature* are the pet words of the pompous, the long-winded, and the empty-headed. They are nearly always redundant. *In a polite manner* means "politely." *Comprehensive in nature* (or *of a comprehensive nature*) means "comprehensively."

To use *manner* and *nature* in phrases like those above is to indicate one of two things: you are deliberately padding a sentence, or you have deluded yourself into thinking such phrases sound dignified. In either case, the effect is annoying.

All redundancies are annoying, *manner* and *nature* especially so because they seem to have a special aura of priggishness all their own. Put the words in dialogue and you can hear the priggishness:

> He: Do you like jazz?
> She: I find it very exciting in nature.

And that should be enough to nip a beautiful friendship in the bud. (Of course, it could be worse. She might have said, "I think that type playing is very exciting in nature, music-wise." But that's really too depressing to think about.)

Drop these stilted, unnecessary *manner* and *nature* phrases altogether. In fact, it might be a good idea to drop the words *manner* and *nature* altogether. Pretend they don't exist. You can get along without them perfectly well; and if they aren't in your vocabulary, you will never be tempted to use them in a phrase.

Drop all of the Terrible Three. Put them behind you forever. Then you can devote your energies to locating and cleaning out the remaining twenty-seven of the thirty abominations. They are listed below. Read them over carefully. Sensitize yourself to them. Become *aware*. That's half the battle.

The Troublesome Twenty-Seven

1. as far as: Must be followed by "is concerned" or it is meaningless.

> *As far as studying is concerned, I've worked hard.* (*Not:* "As far as studying, I've worked hard.")

2. center around: Not possible. You can only center *on*.

3. different: Things are different *from* each other. Don't write *different than*. It makes no sense, just as it would make no sense to write, "I want my books kept separate than the others." Different from, *from*, FROM.

4. *disinterested/uninterested:* The two words mean two different things, and the distinction is valuable. Preserve it. To be *disinterested* is to be impartial. If you are disinterested, you are interested but your emotions are not involved. If you take no interest, you are *uninterested*.

5. *due to:* A graceless phrase, even when used correctly, and it is almost never used correctly. Avoid it altogether.

6. *enthuse:* A word reserved strictly for gushy girls of thirteen or under. Don't use it.

7. *fabulous:* A word ruined by overuse. It means "imaginary, mythical, legendary." You probably hear daily of fabulous cars, fabulous neckties, fabulous meatballs. Unless you want to sound like a movie ad-writer or a professional teenager, drop the word from your vocabulary.

8. *feel bad:* If you are sick or unhappy, you feel *bad*. Not *badly*.

9. *fewer/less:* *Fewer* refers to numbers, *less* to amounts. Don't use *less* in reference to anything you can count: *fewer students, less time, fewer problems, less trouble*.

10. *imply/infer:* To *imply* means to suggest or indicate: "Are you implying that he can't be trusted?" (Are you suggesting that . . .?) To *infer* means to draw a conclusion from: "I didn't say that; you inferred it." (That's what you drew from my statement.)

11. *indefinite pronouns (each, everyone, everybody, either, neither, nobody):* All these pronouns are singular and must be treated consistently as singular. You wouldn't write "Everybody are taking their own lunch," so you shouldn't write "Everybody is taking their own lunch." *Their* is plural. The sentence should be, "Everybody is taking *his* own lunch."

Check out every indefinite pronoun by trying *he* or *she* in its place. If the rest of the sentence agrees with *he* or *she*, it will agree with the indefinite pronoun.

Each of the girls wants her own way. (*Not:* their own way.)

Everyone said he would be on time. (*Not: they* would be on time.)

Everybody in town is having his house painted. (*Not: their* house.)

Neither of the boys is capable of taking proper care of himself. (*Not: themselves*. And note the singular verb: "Neither . . . *is*.")

Nobody will do more than is expected of him. (*Not: them*.)

If a sentence sounds too fussy and pedantic when you follow this rule for indefinite pronouns, recast the sentence. Don't break the rule; outwit it.

12. irregardless: Never to be used, regardless of how many times you hear it said by people who should know better. The word is *regardless*. The *ir-* is redundant; it means the same thing as the *-less* on the end of the word. Saying "irregardless" is rather like saying "irreckless" or "irruthless." Obviously irridiculousless.

13. like/as: Don't use *like* when you mean *as* or *as if.* "Smudgies taste good like a cigaret should" is part of the new television illiteracy. You can avoid wrong usage if you substitute *as though, as if, as,* or *in the way* wherever one of these will make sense in place of *like:*

She acts like a queen. (No substitute is possible here, so *like* is used correctly.)

She acts like she thinks she's a queen. (A substitute would work here, so use it: She acts *as though* she thinks she's a queen.)

She acts like a queen would act. (Use another substitute: She acts *in the way* a queen would act.)

Never use *like* if one of the substitute phrases will work in its place. Test every *like* this way, and you can't be trapped into the wrong usage.

14. mixed metaphor: Don't mix one metaphor with another. The result may be unintentionally comic:

He climbed the ladder of success across a sea of troubles, and left his footprint on the face of time.

You've buttered your bread; now lie in it.

15. off: Always *off;* never *off of.*

16. perfect/unique: If a thing is perfect, it's perfect. If it's unique, it's unique. It can't be *more perfect* (the Founding Fathers notwithstanding) or *more unique.* Perfection and uniqueness are absolute, therefore beyond comparison. Never use "more" or "most" with them.

17. plus: Do not use in place of *and.* Don't say "He was hungry, plus he was penniless." Save *plus* for problems in addition.

18. redundancies: Cut any word that repeats a meaning or that pads without adding anything. Each of the italicized words or phrases below is redundant:

a distance of ten yards	*future* prospects
advanced *forward*	in addition, he *also*
an *actual* fact	inside *of*
another *one*	outside *of*
at *the* present *time*	*past* history
equally as good as	retreat *back*
false illusion	small *in size*
few *in number*	*usual* custom
free gift	*young* teen-ager

These are only a few of the redundancies that clutter English usage. Look for others in your own writing, and avoid them.

19. regarding: Often misused. "Regarding meals, the cafeteria will be open at noon." (The cafeteria seems to be regarding the meals.) The easiest way to avoid this error is to avoid the word "regarding" altogether. Even correctly used it tends to sound like committee language.

20. similar to: If you mean *like,* say *like.* Why beat around the bush?

21. slang: Avoid it like the plague. Some students use it in the mistaken notion that it will make their writing sound informal. It won't. It will merely make it sound juvenile. Or "cute." Nothing is more repulsive in writing than cuteness.

22. so: Don't use it as a substitute for *very* or *terribly* or any other intensifier, as in "Exercise is so exhausting." You can get by with this in speech but not in writing. A reader expects a *so* in this position to be followed by *that:* "Exercise is so exhausing that . . ."

23. split infinitive: Don't put an abverb between the two parts of an infinitive: "to *really* think," "to *positively* believe," "to *suddenly* stop." Put the adverb before or after the infinitive. Better yet, leave it out altogether or recast the sentence.

24. the reason is: Never say "the reason is because . . ." And don't be fooled if other words come in between: "The reason for all these delays is because . . ." Instead, write:

> The reason is that . . .
> The reason for all these delays is that . . .

Or leave out the word "reason" and let "because" do the work:

> This happened. That happened. Because of these delays . . .

√ **25. trite expressions:** Avoid the stale, ready-made expressions that have become overfamiliar and tiresome through constant use by second-rate speakers and third-rate writers. The following list of trite expressions is far from exhaustive, but it's representative:

acid test	green with envy
as luck would have it	last but not least
better late than never	Mother Nature
bitter end	needless to say
busy as a bee	rich and varied experience
depths of despair	ripe old age
easier said than done	sadder but wiser
festive occasion	slow but sure
few and far between	untold agony
finer things in life	words cannot express

26. try: Don't use *try and* when you mean *try to.* "I will try and be there" means that you are planning to do two things —you're going to try, and you're going to be there. You probably mean "I will try *to* be there."

27. while: One of the most misused words in the student vocabulary. It means "time" or "at the time." Never use it as a substitute for *and, but,* or *although.*

> Tolstoi was a Russian writer, while Hemingway was an American writer. (Not possible. Tolstoi died when Hemingway was twelve years old. The writer means "Tolstoi was a Russian writer, *and* Hemingway was an American writer.")

Use *while* only if you can pull it out and substitute *at the time* in its place. Then you can't go wrong.

Punctuation

Punctuation is not really a matter of style; it is a matter of necessity. Without it a writer's sentences would run together in one long toneless hum like this without any of the tones of speech for much of speech is made up of pauses of hesitations of small delays and full stops and it is punctuation that must supply writing with these small necessary silences without them it would take a reader twice as long to extract the meaning from anything he read and he would probably give up in anger or despair or else go quite mad from the din as his inner ear shrieked stop wait what was that you can see perhaps from this how difficult reading can be without punctuation.

In short, the only purpose of punctuation is to make reading easier.

Most punctuation indicates some kind of pause—the kind of pause you would use if you were speaking your sentences instead of writing them. A period, for example, indicates a full stop after a completed thought. The voice falls. The sentence is finished. That's it. Period.

Commas indicate the small pauses *inside* the sentence. *Listen to your sentences.* A natural pause usually means that you need a comma:

> After all, the man was no fool. (Hear the pause after *all?*)
>
> She may be pretty, but she's mean. (Hear the pause after *pretty?*)
>
> He bought beans, potatoes, salt, flour, and onions. (Hear the pauses?)
>
> He will also buy, if he is wise, a slab of bacon. (Hear the pauses?)

Failure to indicate pauses can lead to complete confusion. Look at the difference one small comma can make:

> Did the cat eat Mary?
> Did the cat eat, Mary?
> Percy, the cat has run away.
> Percy, the cat, has run away.

For every kind of pause natural to speech, written language has a corresponding mark of punctuation. Your ear alone can usually guide you to the proper use of periods and commas, as they are demonstrated in the examples given here, but your ear is not enough to guide you in the use of all the markings.

Particularly the semicolon. Special attention must be called to it because so many students seem to suffer from semicolonitis; semicolons break out like measles all over the face of their compositions. Apparently this is caused by a widespread belief that a semicolon is a kind of dignified comma. It is not. And it cannot be used in place of a comma. It's a kind of lightweight period, to be used only between closely related and evenly balanced complete thoughts. Don't use it at random, tossing it into a pause just because you like the look of it. Honor the semicolon, and keep it wholly for the purpose it was created to serve.

You should know, out of simple courtesy toward readers as well as respect for your own work, the proper use of all the other punctuation marks—colons, dashes, hyphens, apostrophes, parentheses, brackets, ellipses, quotation marks. All these are conventions established by long usage to mean certain highly specific things.

Consult your grammar text. Learn all the fine distinctions. You will be surprised to find out how expressive a mere mark of the pen can be.

Summary

The thirty transgressions listed in this chapter are not the only sins against style, but they are the most common—and the most likely to cause offense to the discriminating reader. The easiest way to handle them at first is to forget about them until you are ready to write the final draft of your paper. Then check. And check closely. Go through your entire paper, checking every sentence against every item on the list until you are certain you have rid yourself completely of the thirty offenders.

It may be a slow, laborious process at first, and you will probably be appalled at how many items from the list show up in your writing. But gradually you will find that control has become automatic; you will find fewer and fewer of the thirty barbarisms in your work because your heightened awareness of them will help you avoid them from the start. Habit will take over. The deliberate, painstaking, conscious hunting-down of stylistic faults leads eventually to a natural, almost unconscious avoidance of those faults.

The Terrible Three probably won't give you much trouble.

They are so laughably obvious, once you have become sensitized to them, that they will probably disappear from your writing immediately. (They will also provide you with a fine source of private amusement as you discover how often *-wise* and *type of* and *manner* or *nature* turn up in the speech and writing of people who should know better.)

The remaining twenty-seven stylistic faults are slyer and more persistent, but these too will eventually disappear as your awareness increases—as it will, if you are vigilant.

In any case, checking over your paper for the barbarisms listed in this chapter is a very slight effort indeed compared to the effort you have already put into your essay. You have gone to the hard labor of creating something entirely new and entirely your own. Before you send it out to face the world, give it this final grooming. You owe that to yourself.

QUESTIONS

1. Notice the title of this chapter. What play on words do you find in it, and how does it relate to the content of this chapter?
2. What are the "Terrible Three"? Give an example of each.
3. Why is the phrase "center around" a logical impossibility?
4. Why is "fabulous" a poor word to use in most writing?
5. Logically, what is meant by "I feel badly"?
6. What is wrong with the word "irregardless"?
7. What test can you give the word "like" to make certain that you are using it correctly?
8. Why is it impossible to be "more perfect" or "more unique"?
9. What is a trite expression? Give examples other than those in the text.
10. Explain the real purpose of punctuation and illustrate its relation to sound.
11. What kind of pause does a comma indicate?
12. Explain the proper use of the semicolon.

ASSIGNMENT

1. Write three sentences using the suffix *-wise* as it should *not* be used. Then rewrite the sentence without the suffix.

Example: Everything was against him, percentage-wise.
All the percentages were against him.

2. Write three sentences using the expression "type" or "type of." Then rewrite correctly.
3. Write three sentences using the expressions "in nature," "of a . . . nature," and "in a . . . manner." Then rewrite correctly.
4. Write a sentence that demonstrates, in the same order listed in the chapter, each of the stylistic flaws in the "Troublesome Twenty-Seven." Then after each sentence that contains the flaw, rewrite to get rid of the flaw.

Example: As far as exercise, few people get enough.
As far as exercise is concerned, few people get enough.

5. Find the stylistic flaw in each of the sentences below and rewrite the sentence correctly. Some sentences contain more than one flaw.

a. Everybody who came to the meeting thought the discussion ought to center around their particular problem.
b. While he was not a doctor, he was very well informed as far as treatments for sore throat.
c. The course was different than he expected.
d. He acted like he was green with envy.
e. Just to be sure of impartiality, get an uninterested judge for the contest.
f. Regarding his future prospects, they look good.
g. If he would get off of that subject, he could make a lot of forward progress inside of a year.
h. It was the most perfect kind of response to a silly question.
i. Your letter seems to infer that you are ready to retreat back from your former position.
j. He felt badly about it, but it was all past history now, and outside of expressing his regrets he could do nothing but try and keep things under better control in the future ahead.
k. Each of the girls are asked to seriously consider the risks of the program.
l. She was too disinterested in the subject to attend the lecture, plus she was certain it would be similar to all the other lectures she had heard.
m. The movie was fabulous, but due to closing hours she had to leave before it ended.
n. He knew he might have false illusions about his ability, but he decided to enter the contest irregardless.

o. He found the hike so exhausting, and the reason was because he had slept for only a short period of time the night before.

6. On page 152, under "Punctuation," is an entire paragraph that contains no punctuation after the first sentence. Beginning with the second sentence, copy the entire paragraph and punctuate it correctly.

13

More Freedom and a Few Flourishes

You have been held, so far, to the rather tight structure of reasoned argument. Hopefully, this discipline has taught you to *think* structurally, so that you can try your hand at any kind of essay—from the most serious to the most lighthearted, the most personal to the most detached—without having it fall apart.

You have also been held to the limitation of writing all your essays in third person. Hopefully again, this has given you greater control than you might otherwise have achieved over certain elements of style. You have earned the right at last to use first person. You have even earned the right to admit the word "there" into your writing vocabulary again. You have served a rigorous apprenticeship. Freedom lies ahead.

Now it is time for fresh explorations, for experiment, for lighthearted adventure. For of course not all essays are solemn exercises in logical argument and persuasion; some are highly personal and anecdotal, ranging in tone from tragic to comic. Others are so subtle and urbane that only the most perceptive reader is aware of their underlying structure; they seem less like organized works of composition than direct encounters with the writer's personality. The more essays you read—and the more experiments you make—the more you will become aware of the tremendous range of possibilities in the essay form.

Following are four specific assignments, each designed to teach you something new or to give you practice in a particular technique. All of them should give you pleasure. If you have chafed at the restrictions hitherto imposed, if you have felt impatient and earthbound, take heart. You are about to take flight.

Assignment 1: First Person at Last

Using first person, write an essay based on a personal experience. This time, instead of developing your thesis with *pro* and *con* argument, you will develop it by telling a story. You will tell it in much the same way you would tell it to a friend and for the same reason: because it is something that really happened to you, and because it proves your point.

It may be something that happened years ago or the day before yesterday. Try to re-create in your writing the look and sound and feel of the experience. An important part of the assignment is the creation of scene through concrete detail, so that the reader is aware not only of your emotional reaction to the event but aware also of its setting in a real world of real textures and colors and sounds.

Usually your memory will serve up exactly the right kind of physical detail in connection with any important experience; but if you can remember only the emotional impact of an event and none of the details, use your imagination. Were you lost as a child in a railway station? Then create in your mind a picture of how it must have been or could have been—the torn poster on a wall, the tremble in the air as a train approached, the hum of strange voices, the smell of leather or peanuts or perfume or wet wool, the acid taste of your own fright. Be specific. Make things real.

Most importantly, however, choose an experience that has some meaning for you. Description alone is empty; it has no dramatic impact. A meaningful experience is one that has influenced you in some way. It may be an exciting experience or a very quiet one, but looking back at it you can see that it helped make you into the kind of person you are. It left you with an *opinion* of some kind about human nature or about society or simply about life. And that opinion is your thesis.

Suppose, for example, that you choose to write about a childhood experience with racial prejudice. You may have seen some cruel or thoughtless act that you could not understand at the time. You may have committed such an act yourself. Or you may have been its victim. In any case, you have never forgotten the incident. It clings stubbornly to your memory, and the fact that it does cling is proof enough that it has influenced you, led you to adopt certain opinions. Your thesis could be that a bad conscience lasts a lifetime, or that children learn prejudice by example, or that unconscious cruelty can be worse than open enmity. It could be any number of other things, depending upon your experience.

Introduce your thesis just as you would introduce it in a standard essay—by opening with a generalization that leads up to it gradually. Avoid the use of the word "I" in your opening remarks. Hold it until you are ready to state your thesis.

> *The paradox of writing in first person is that although you use the word "I" to tell your story, you are not really writing about yourself.*

You are writing about an *experience;* the "I" is simply there for naturalness. Your reader will be interested in the experience and in the conclusion you have drawn from it, but he will not really be interested in *you.* The slightest suspicion of self-aggrandizement, in fact, is enough to make his lip curl.

Consider, for example, the overpowering self-esteem of the writer below, who is much more interested in talking about herself than about her subject:

> I am a very sensitive person and have been ever since I was a little girl. I cannot stand cruelty of any kind. I was just a child when I saw my first example of racial prejudice, and it had a deep effect on me, for even then I could see that it was cruel. To me, the most important thing in the world is kindness . . .

The young lady who wrote this is, of course, kidding herself. The most important thing in the world is herself. And you may be certain that in any personal experience she recounts she will emerge as the heroine—modest, misunderstood, martyred, sweetly protesting, but always the heroine. She will also always be a bore, and nobody could tolerate her for five minutes.

So concentrate on the experience, not on your *self.* Be honest. Set it all down as truthfully as you can, letting the reader see it for himself and interpret it for himself. Don't worry about impressing him with your sterling qualities; if you have them, they will show through in your writing without any assistance on your part. If you don't have them, you only prove it by insisting upon them. It is the judgment you have made of your experience, not the experience itself, that will demonstrate the quality of your mind, and that is all the reader wants to know about you.

After you have stated your thesis, move immediately into your story, telling it in the same natural sequence you would use if you were telling it in conversation, but using all the art at your command in the use of specific detail and figurative language. Don't moralize. Don't preach. You have made your point in the thesis sentence. Let the story itself carry it out without any further comment.

It will conclude itself naturally. You need not go back to the introductory paragraph for a key to the conclusion. Just end your story, perhaps with one or two lines rather than a full paragraph:

> Somehow I never felt the same about Uncle Charlie after that.

If Uncle Charlie, in the course of your story, has done something that has influenced your values, the reader will get the point. You will only dull it if you add a moral tag or an explanation.

Assignment 2: How to Write Badly by Trying Very, Very Hard

You have spent a great part of the year learning how to improve your writing by using active verbs and concrete detail, by avoiding vague abstractions, clichés, and redundancies. Now you are going to kick over the traces by writing an essay that deliberately violates all these principles.

You are to be luxuriously long-winded, devastatingly dull, overpoweringly pompous.

You may write in first person or third, but you must stick carefully to standard structure, for your essay must appear to be highly, even loftily, reasoned. Pick a thesis so trivial and/or obvious that nobody in his right mind would consider arguing it—something like "The adhesive quality of adhesive tape is frequently so sticky in nature that it produces negative reactions, skin-wise" or "The standardization of electric-type signals has been important safety-wise in the solution of problems of traffic."

The whole point is to do deliberately some of the very things you have learned *not* to do. Now is your chance to get them out of your system. Don't try to be funny (that will take care of itself). And don't violate *all* the principles of good style—if you do that, your paper will be unreadable. Just follow the rules below:

1. Use only passive voice (no active or "audio-visual" verbs at all).

2. Use the *-wise* suffix at least twice in every paragraph.

3. Use *type, type of,* and *manner* or *nature* phrases as often as possible.

4. Use abstractions, preferably in every sentence: important-sounding words ending in *-tion, -ment, -ance, -ence, -ism, -ness, -ity,* and *-acy.*

5. Inflate simple statements. Don't say "He looked bad." Say "He had the appearance of being in an unhealthy condition." Don't say "He did good work." Say "The type work accomplished by him was excellent in nature."

6. Use every trite expression you can think of (see list on page 151 if you run short).

Don't use slang. Don't violate any of the other principles you have learned. Just use the six rules listed above. The result will be a parody. To give your essay an even stronger satiric thrust, insert an occasional very short, very direct, very down-to-earth statement into the mainstream of overblown sentences:

> It is a well-known fact that the application of tape of an adhesive nature to an individual's epidermis has a tendency to produce a rash-type reaction, skin-wise. When such tape is used on areas that are large in size, it frequently produces in conjunction with the rash certain sensations of a burning and stinging nature that are a source of discomfort to an intense degree. In short, it makes you itch.

Develop your points with ponderous, unsmiling seriousness. Wind up your essay with a conclusion that matches the grandiose cloudiness of your introduction, including a resounding cliché and perhaps some portentous reference to the state of the world—something with the unfailing banality of "a better world in which to live" or "the ever-increasing complexity of modern-type life."

By all means treat yourself to at least one class session devoted to reading these papers aloud, just to share the fun. You might even offer the best-worst essay some kind of prize —perhaps a document, suitable for framing, bearing every student's signature and favorite cliché.

Assignments 3 and 4: Irony

> *Irony is the art of using words that say one thing and mean another. Its purpose, however, is not to deceive but to make clear.*

It is at once the subtlest and the most necessary of the essayist's skills, for every essay needs a touch of irony. Without it, writing is like bread made without salt—nutritious but unappetizing.

You are perfectly familiar with irony. You glance out the window at a desolate February landscape whipped by a freezing rain and remark, "I love these fresh spring days." That's irony. Or you say, yawning, when the score of the ball game stands at 35–0 and the whole crowd is paralyzed with boredom, "I'm not sure I can stand all this excitement." That's irony. By saying what you don't mean, you make doubly clear what you do mean. The weather is awful, the game is utterly dull. Everybody gets the point.

The ironic essay is simply an extension of this kind of meaning-in-reverse.

The range of irony in writing, however, is enormous. An essay may be fully and openly ironic, or it may have only ironic undertones. Your writing experiments this time, therefore, require two assignments. You are to write two essays—one sweepingly ironic, the other bearing only the touch of irony. The big sweep comes first; it should prepare you to handle the subtleties.

THE FULLY IRONIC ESSAY

Choose a thesis as you would choose it for any essay. Then reverse it and *overstate* it. That overstatement is important; it's the signal to your reader that your words are not to be taken at face value.

Suppose, for example, that your family dotes on outdoor camping, and you loathe it. Real thesis: Outdoor camping is terrible. Ironic thesis: Outdoor camping is one of life's greatest delights. (Every infected mosquito bite brings back beautiful memories. The hours spent in an oxygen tent, recovering from pneumonia, are a small price to pay for those nights in a spider-infested sleeping bag under the dripping pines . . .)

Or suppose that a group of students has been guilty of extremely bad sportsmanship at an important game. Real thesis: Such behavior is inexcusable. Ironic thesis: Such behavior shows true nobility of spirit. (The so-called guilty students are really clean-cut young heroes who deserve some special award for gallantry. They have handled a problem in the American Way, with their fists and with colorful native American language, and any criticism of them is disloyal, if not downright subversive. The bad publicity resulting from their actions merely proves the narrow-minded incompetence of the local press.)

Or suppose that some group in your community is pressuring the school to remove certain books from the library. Real thesis: Their action can set a dangerous precedent for any special-interest group choosing to limit the spirit of free inquiry. Ironic thesis: Their action shows a revival of the real American community spirit. (Book burnings can take the place of the old-fashioned barbecue or barn dance. Why not have weekly bonfires until all the library books are gone, and then toss in all the textbooks in one great culminating blaze? And think of the economic advantages—no need to pay a librarian, no need even to pay teachers, eventually, since they will probably all leave. But who needs schools anyway? The buildings can be turned into jails for the troublemakers who still believe that books serve a useful purpose in life.)

From the most playful kind of thesis to the most serious, the technique is the same: put your thesis into reverse in exaggerated terms and develop an argument that seems to praise while it actually attacks.

In short, say what you mean by saying what you don't mean. Don't try to be funny—that will take care of itself. And don't attack personalities—that's cheap sarcasm, not irony. For serious essays, stick to ideas, policies, programs; for the merely humorous, use the nuisances and discomforts and absurdities of life for your subject matter. Always present your mock thesis as though it makes complete and admirable good sense. Develop it in the same way, with arguments that are perfectly logical in relation to your mock thesis, however outrageous they may seem if judged by ordinary standards.

In your own phrase, play it cool. Then you will have irony.

THE IRONIC TOUCH

Now that you have experimented with the big, bold design of the completely ironic essay, it is time to refine your skill, to learn how to give your writing the ironic touch rather than the full ironic treatment. This is perhaps the most valuable skill you can learn, for you will seldom be called upon to wage the kind of total war to which total irony is committed, but you will very often be called upon to write straightforward exposition or description in which a touch of irony can mean the difference between ordinariness and distinction.

You must understand, first of all, that irony does not necessarily mean all-out attack. It is a part of all writing that has real grace, even when no controversy is involved. A brief ironic reference, for example, can give a lift to flatly factual material:

> For several years Mason lived in Boggsville, where literature meant the mail-order catalog and art meant the feed-store calendar. He left in 1942.

So far, no irony. "He left in 1942" is a perfectly colorless statement of fact. Even if you wrote, "He was glad to be able to leave in 1942," you would have no irony. But a very casual overstatement can change it:

> He escaped from this paradise in 1942.

You realize instantly that the writer considers Boggsville anything but a paradise. "You and I know, of course," he seems to be saying "that Boggsville was a dreadful hole, and Mason was a lucky man to get away from the place." In effect, the writer pays you a subtle compliment by trusting you to understand what he really means. Compare the effect of "He escaped from this paradise" with "He was glad to be able to leave," and the latter seems insultingly flat and obvious.

This use of irony to avoid the statement of the obvious is, by the way, one of its pleasantest uses. It can convert even a sentence that verges on downright simple-mindedness into a literary asset. The raw beginner, for example, might end a paragraph that described some action by a cold and arrogant man like this: "This proves that he had no feeling for others." The writer with the ironic touch would write, "It was a typically warmhearted gesture." One wry comment, one reversal of the obvious, and the whole paragraph has a new tone.

The ironic touch never calls attention to itself. It appears suddenly and is gone, like a quick, secret smile between two people in a crowded room. It may be no more than the small, pleasant shock of surprise brought about by an apparently incongruous relationship between words. Where the unskilled writer would use an overworked adjective like "awful," the ironic writer will speak of a "dedicated bore," an "inspired gossip," an "unswerving coward." And because words like *dedicated, inspired* and *unswerving* are usually associated with quite respectable activities, they provide a minor reversal that pleases because it surprises.

Opportunity after opportunity for irony presents itself in essay writing. Its uses cannot be prescribed; they are too subtle and too various. Irony, in fact, is more than a literary technique; it is a quality of mind. You must teach yourself to stand at some distance from your subject, to translate your private judgments and observations ("That must have been some paradise!" and "What a mean thing to do!") into the kind of cool, detached statement suitable for the essay. Oddly enough, this coolness is chiefly responsible for the personal quality that forges the warmest of all bonds between reader and writer; this is another of the paradoxes of writing. Perhaps it happens because the reader, sensing the personality of the writer behind the words, often feels that he has met a kindred soul, someone who feels as he does about things, and he delights in recognizing secret signals from a friend.

Irony succeeds, of course, only when the reader is "in" on the secret. You must be quite certain, when you say what you don't mean, that your reader knows you don't mean it. If he takes you seriously, you're in trouble. (Imagine, for example, how indignant he would be if he thought you *seriously* advocated bad sportsmanship, or what a fool he would consider you if he thought you *really* looked upon Boggsville as a paradise.) Be sure, always, to give your reader enough clues to remind him constantly of the real meaning behind your words.

It would be interesting, for this assignment, to rewrite one of your earliest essays (if it is still available) to see how much it can be improved by an infusion of irony. Otherwise, choose any serious thesis that interests you. Write your introduction without any attempt at irony. Keep your development straightforward, but try to give every paragraph at least a touch of irony—one surprising conjunction of words, one ironic reference, or one gently ironic comment.

The result should be the best essay you have written.

QUESTIONS

1. How do you arrive at a thesis for an essay about a personal experience?

2. How does the development of this thesis differ from the development of the thesis in an essay of argument?

3. Suppose you write a colorful description of a city street scene, using first person throughout. Is this an essay? Explain your answer.

4. Why is the use of the word "I" usually paradoxical? Under what circumstances would it *not* be paradoxical?

5. What is a "moral tag"? Give an example of the kind of moral tag that might appear at the end of the suggested essay on racial prejudice. Why would it be a mistake?

6. What is the chief value of "writing badly by trying very, very hard"?

7. What is irony? What is the chief principle underlying it?

8. How does the fully ironic essay differ from the essay that has only the ironic touch?

9. How can you make certain that a reader understands that you are being ironic? Give an example other than any of those in this chapter.

14

Writing the Term Paper

The ability to write a satisfactory term paper (or research paper, as it is often called) is an absolute requirement for academic success in college, where it is as standard a part of almost every course as the lecture or the final examination. Entirely apart from this very practical consideration, however, the experience of writing the term paper has tremendous value for any student. It can open up whole new avenues of learning. In fact, you can probably learn more, and learn it faster, with a stronger sense of intellectual satisfaction, by writing a term paper than by any other method. Provided, of course, that you understand what you are doing and go about it in the right way.

Unfortunately, many students—both in college and in high school—think of the term paper as simply a long, tiresome report that is supposed to prove, if it proves anything, that they have done outside reading on their subject. To this end they visit the library and industriously copy enough more-or-less related facts from various reference books to meet the requirement ("Miss Thompson said eight pages, didn't she?"), gather the result under a handsome title page bearing the legend "Term Paper" (which is supposed to make it official), and hand it in with a large sigh of relief, secretly convinced that the whole enterprise has been a complete waste of time.

The conviction is well founded. Any resemblance between this kind of dutiful copy work and a real term paper is purely coincidental, and you may rest assured that Miss Thompson will be as bored with it as you are.

So perhaps you should get one thing straight first of all: you don't write a term paper just to prove you have done time in the library. And you don't write it to show Miss Thompson how neatly you can copy excerpts from the *Britannica*. Or even how cagily you can "rewrite in your own words" the ideas of other writers.

You write a term paper to *express your own opinion* on a chosen topic, and you go to the library because that's where you will find the facts to back up your opinion—and the arguments, both for and against it, that have been put forward by other writers. You don't steal their arguments. You compare them, with each other and with your own, and you look for something new to say on the subject, even if it's only to raise a question or make a judgment on what has already been said.

A term paper, in other words, is an essay. It's a highly specialized form of the essay, with certain extra rules of its own, but it is nevertheless an essay, with all the requirements for structure and style that the word suggests. And that means that it requires, first and foremost and above all, a *thesis*.

The Trial Thesis

You should have a tentative, or trial, thesis in mind even before you make your first trip to the library.

This will be easy enough if you can pick your own topic for a term paper. Your own interest will guide you in taking a position. If your topic is assigned, formulate a thesis just as you would for any essay (look back on page 26 if you have forgotten how). You can do this even though you know very little about your topic.

Suppose, for example, that you must do a paper on automation for your course in Modern Problems. You know only that automation involves the use of machines and electronic devices to do work that has always been done previously by human labor and that some people fear it because it takes jobs away from men. You might begin with a trial thesis like this: "Automation will never be widespread enough to create serious unemployment problems." You really have no idea whether that is true or not. But at least you have a place to start. You know what kind of information to look for.

Your trial thesis, right or wrong, gives your work a guiding purpose. As you search for evidence to support your view, you may change your mind completely. That's fine. In fact, it will make your final thesis stronger than ever simply because you understand both sides of the question and can speak with greater conviction on the side you eventually choose.

When you have picked a trial thesis, you are ready to start your research. Unlike the short, personal essay that can come "straight out of your head," the term paper requires that you back up your thesis with a thorough investigation of the facts and of the opinions put forward by experts. You can borrow from the experts freely to support your case, but *you must always make sure that your reader knows you are borrowing.* You must credit your sources: Jones says this, Poindexter believes that, Mungle has such-and-such in mind.

It is very bad manners—in fact, it is downright theft—to use the words of other men as your own, even though you rewrite them beyond recognition. Always give credit where credit is due. When you quote an author, you must let the reader know his full name, the name of the publication in which you found the material that you quote, even the exact page number. Certain standard methods of quoting, footnoting, and listing exist precisely for this purpose. They are the conventions of research, and they must be followed to the letter. That means you must keep very careful records of everything you read.

To help make the whole business as easy as possible, experienced researchers have worked out a very definite and almost foolproof procedure that includes even such minute details as the proper measurements of a note card. If you have never done research before, such details are likely to strike you as unimportant. But, as many a grieving student in the last gray hours of the term has learned to his sorrow, they are very important indeed. So follow every detail of the procedure exactly, no matter how trivial you believe it to be. You will save yourself a great deal of trouble.

Procedure for Research

When you go to the library to take notes, take the following equipment with you:

1. A stack of 3″ x 5″ note cards, or slightly larger cards if you have outsize handwriting. (You may use slips of paper cut to size if you prefer, but cards are easier to handle and they have a good solid feeling that is very reassuring.)

2. A reliable pen. (*Never* take notes with a pencil. Those cards are going to take some punishment, and you want legible notes, not useless smudges.)

3. A rubber band, or a stout manila envelope made to fit your cards. (Don't risk losing even one card; it can cost you hours of work. Keep all of them together, always.)

Your first step is to locate your material. Consult the following, in this order:

1. The *Encyclopædia Britannica* (or any other reliable encyclopedia if this is not available).
2. The card catalog.
3. *Reader's Guide to Periodical Literature.*
4. *Essay and General Literature Index.*

The encyclopedia. This will supply you with solid background in your subject which, in turn, will help you understand more fully everything else you read. Take brief notes, paying special attention to anything in the entry that bears particularly on your trial thesis. Make special note of the list of authorities and their works at the end of the entry; you should know the names of experts in your subject and take a look at their works if they are available.

In all probability you won't quote anything at all from the encyclopedia in your term paper. The notes you take from it are mainly to help you keep in mind a body of facts about your subject, and it is seldom necessary to supply footnotes for such facts, since they are part of a body of general information.

The card catalog. This will supply you with a list of the books available in your library on your subject. Look under your subject heading ("automation," for example) and *fill out a separate 3 x 5 card* for each book that looks promising. Put the call number in the upper left-hand corner. That's for your own information. Alongside it goes the information needed for your term paper: author, title, publisher, and date of publication. It will look like this:

> 301.243
> B455
>
> Berkeley, Edmund C.
> The Computer Revolution
> (Doubleday, 1962).

Always underline book titles (this indicates italics). When you finally have the book in your hands, check your card to make certain that it contains accurately all the information you will need for footnoting and bibliography (see pages 176–179). A note in time may save you an extra trip to the library.

Readers' Guide to Periodical Literature. This is an index to the contents of over two hundred magazines, and it is indispensable to research. One fat volume is published every year; you will usually find all the volumes together, lined up chronologically, at some central point in the library. In addition to the full-year volumes, paperback supplements are published regularly during the current year to keep the listings up to date. Look for your subject heading—"automation," for example —and you will find a complete list of everything published on your subject in the selected magazines, with precise information on author, title of article, name of publication, date, and page number.

Start with the current year and drop back to earlier years for additional listings. With a rather new subject like automation, you will probably find more material in periodicals than in books. A large body of literature in book form simply has not had time to develop. You might like to check the gradual growth of interest in the subject as it is reflected in the number of articles published about it and to see whether any changes in emphasis have taken place—in fact, this might in itself be a topic for a term paper.

Keeping your thesis in mind, list all likely-looking articles that appear under your subject heading, taking special care to include not only those that support your thesis but also those that seem to argue against it. Remember, you have not yet formed a final judgment and should not do so until you have looked at both sides of the question.

Again, use a *separate card* for each article that you plan to look up. Just inside the cover of *Reader's Guide* you will find a key to all the abbreviations in the listings. Refer to this key, and spell out all the abbreviations in full on your card—otherwise, you may be lost when you are ready to track down the publication. Record everything shown on the card that follows: author, title of article, title of magazine, volume number, date, page numbers:

```
305
M582.
Hilton, Alice Mary

    "Cyberculture — the Age of Abundance
and Leisure," Michigan Quarterly
Review, III (Fall, 1964), 217-229.
```

Any periodical old enough to be bound and in the stacks will have a call number. Consult the card catalog, under the name of the periodical.

Pay particular attention to the punctuation when you write your card entry. The title of the article is in quotation marks, the magazine title is underlined, the volume number is in Roman numerals and is *not* followed by a comma, the month and year are in parentheses and separated from the page numbers by a comma. Follow this form *exactly*. If you do it right the first time, you will have fewer worries when you prepare your final bibliography for your term paper.

Essay and General Literature Index. This is an index to thousands of essays and articles from miscellaneous sources that may escape the *Reader's Guide.* Here, for example, are notable articles that have appeared in the scholarly journals and in collections or anthologies of various kinds. Follow exactly the same procedure with this index that you followed with *Reader's Guide:* make out a separate card for each item that you want to look up.

A number of other special-area encyclopedias and indexes are available, and you should acquaint yourself with the full range of reference material carried by your library, particularly if you want to go into your subject in great depth. For most term papers, however, a general encyclopedia, the card catalog, and the two big reference works cited above will suffice.

Just remember that the catalog and all those rather forbidding-looking volumes of reference exist for one purpose: to help you find what you are looking for. Take full advantage of the help they are prepared to give you.

Each of the cards you have filled out so far is a *bibliography card*. (A bibliography is simply a list of published works.) Don't write anything else on these cards. Add other cards when you come across a new title in your reading (you can frequently find something that will be valuable to your own work in the bibliography of another author). But keep the bibliography cards separate from those on which you take your notes.

Start reading and taking notes. Begin with the books in your bibliography. With your thesis in mind every moment, look first through the chapter headings (or the preface, if the book has no chapter headings) to get a grasp of the main ideas and organization. You will be surprised at how quickly you can find what you want when you know what you are looking for. If a book obviously has nothing to offer you, put it aside and go on to the next one.

Take notes sparingly, and never put more than one note on a card, even if the note is so short that most of the card seems to be wasted space. In the upper left corner, write the last name of the author (your bibliography card will supply you with the full name when you need it). In the upper right corner, indicate with a word or two the topic of the note. Notes on automation, for example, might be labeled BENEFITS, DANGERS, LABOR'S VIEW, GOVERNMENT'S ROLE, etc. Your subject and your thesis will automatically dictate these labels; you will find that everything you read tends to fall naturally into certain classifications.

A note may be a summary in your own words of an author's meaning or it may be a quotation taken directly from his work. If it's a quotation, it must be *exactly* as it appears in print and must be enclosed in quotation marks. If you want to put a comment of your own on the same card, enclose your own words in brackets. In any case, be sure to write the page number along with the quotation, whether it is direct or indirect:

UNIONS

Raskin, p. 15

Trend now toward "lifetime jobs" — men can't be forced off jobs because of automation but need not be replaced if they die, retire, or quit voluntarily.

Brief summary in your own words.

Hilton, p. 225   FUTURE (YOUTH)

"Unemployment is swelled less by those who have been fired than by those who are no longer hired." [What happens to high school graduates looking for work?]

Exact quotations plus comment. Note brackets.

When you are summarizing an author's ideas, bear in mind the principles of paragraph structure that you have learned. This will help you to boil some other writer's paragraph down to its essentials and to keep your notes brief. It is pointless to copy a whole paragraph when you intend to refer only to its main idea, so save yourself time (and clarify your own thinking in the process) by asking yourself, before you start to write your note, "What's the main idea here?" Then put it in your own words as concisely as possible.

Never write on both sides of a note card. If you allow yourself to do it even once, you will never be quite certain which card it is when you begin working with the whole collection, and turning over dozens of cards to find one lost detail that may or may not be on the back of one card can be a maddening annoyance and waste of time. Try to keep your notes short enough for one card, but if a note runs over, write "more" in the lower right-hand corner and continue with a fresh card (but make sure it also has the author's name on it and an appropriate notation—*Smith, cont'd 2, Smith, cont'd 3*, etc., and repeat the label you have written in the upper right-hand corner of the first card).

The note-taking procedure is the same for both books and periodicals. Keep your summaries brief, keep your quotations exact, and keep records of source and page numbers accurate.

The Final Thesis

It is possible, even probable, that your trial thesis, or hypothesis, will have undergone some changes during your reading. You were, after all, relatively uninformed when you started your research; it would be rather surprising if your investigations did not lead to at least some slight change in your point of view.

For example, if you had begun with the hypothesis suggested for automation ("Automation will never be widespread enough to create serious unemployment problems"), you would almost certainly have changed your mind after exposure to scientific facts and expert opinion. In fact, you are likely to be staggered by your discoveries about automation and its meaning in your own future. You may decide that the problem is not *whether* automation will bring serious unemployment problems, but *how* these problems should be handled. Or you may find yourself going beyond immediate considerations of employment to a whole range of problems that had never occurred to you before.

You may find yourself asking questions like this: What happens to human beings when work, which has always been at the very foundation of our society, no longer has meaning? What will be the effect on human values? How should a man be trained to live in a society that has no need of his labor?

How does he earn the money to buy the products that machines can turn out without his help? If he cannot work, how is he to spend his time? What is the government's role in this new kind of society?

Automation (particularly the science of cybernetics—roughly, the use of computer-controlled machines that some scientists now coolly predict will take over *all* the work in industry formerly done by human labor) is so new that even the experts have not yet fully explored its startling implications; but on one thing most of them, in both science and industry, seem to be agreed: An electronic revolution, as far-reaching in its effects as the industrial or the agricultural revolution, is already well under way, and vast changes are inevitable. Some believe it will bring a magnificent new age of abundance and freedom; some believe it will destroy society.

Your own judgment, after you have informed yourself *on both sides* of the issue, might be something like this: Although automation will probably result in tremendous material benefits to man, it will also create social problems that should be brought to public attention immediately so that solutions can be studied in advance. And your final thesis will be: "Automation will create social problems . . ."

This is a far cry from your trial thesis. But no matter. That trial thesis had only one purpose: to serve as a probe, an investigative tool that would lead you into a body of information. Once it has served that purpose, discard it if it no longer serves your purpose. Never hesitate to modify a trial thesis if your research causes you to change your mind or sets you off in a slightly different direction.

About midway in your reading, however, you should begin to feel fairly certain of the main point you want to make in your term paper, and your growing conviction about the rightness of one point of view as opposed to any other will, in turn, influence all the rest of your reading—as it becomes more specialized, it will become more meaningful. By the time you are ready to start writing, your thesis must be firm and final. It is a waste of time to start writing until you are absolutely certain of your thesis.

Your Paper Is in the Cards

You should have a sizable stack of note cards by the time you have finished your research. Read through them quickly to get a general impression of the ground you have covered. Then start sorting.

Stack together all the cards that deal with one particular point (the label you wrote in the upper right corner will help here). You will find that some of the stacks are much thicker than others; this probably means that a point needs further division—that is, it will require several paragraphs if it is to be covered fully. With automation, for example, the stack labeled EMPLOYMENT might be divided into several categories —*present trends, available statistics, labor's view, management's view*, etc.

You will also find that your cards fall generally into the *con* and *pro* classification. With your revised thesis on automation ("Automation will create social problems . . ."), *con* cards will be benefits (you *concede* that automation will bring material benefits), *pro* cards will be problems (you are *propounding* the argument that the public needs to be made more aware of the problems). You might note, for example, that people tend to equate automation with such modern devices as change machines, thermostats, self-service laundries, transistorized radios, and direct dialing. *But*—and here you begin to pull in your *pro* points—too few people are aware that a genuine revolution, capable of changing their lives radically, is taking place.

You will, of course, have more *pro* cards than *con* cards. Put all *con* cards together; you will want to deal with these first and get on to your real argument. Then separate all the cards in the *pro* group according to topic, put a rubber band around each stack, and lay them out in the order you will use them in your paper. Remember to put your most telling point last.

What you now have, in effect, is a kind of three-dimensional outline—far more flexible and more easily constructed than a formal written outline, and for most students much more meaningful. The actual handling of the cards, the shuffling and rearranging required to lay them out in the most logical order, is astonishingly effective in helping you establish a firm structure—and you can do it all without the kind of agonizing debate and insecurity that so frequently accompanies the preparation of a formal written outline (Should I use a Roman numeral here? Is this an *A* point or an *a* point? How do I phrase this heading?). The cards will lead you, easily and logically, from one argument to the next. Write your introduction, state your thesis, and then start through your cards, using the information on them to shape your own coherent, fully developed paragraphs, quoting when necessary.

Never attempt to get your paper written simply by transferring information from a card to your manuscript in one undigested lump. The purpose of the material you have gathered on your cards is to *back up* your own judgment, to provide evidence. It is there simply to help you to prove *your* point. So make sure that the central idea in each of your paragraphs is clearly your own and that every scrap of borrowed evidence that you are using is credited to its rightful source.

That means footnotes and bibliography. You will need to write at least two drafts of your paper—a rough one that develops your notes and indicates the position of your footnotes, leaving room for revisions; and a final one that ties everything together, with every detail of documentation complete.

Writing the First Draft

Write your introduction first, but don't spend too much time on it. Remember, you will almost certainly revise it in your final draft. Open with a fairly broad generalization related to your thesis, just as you would with any essay, and narrow gradually toward your thesis. Don't try to pull in references in this first paragraph. You are launching your own thesis in your own words, and footnotes this early would make it appear that you were too unsure of your ground to say anything at all with confidence:

> For centuries men have dreamed of a society in which machines did all the work and men were freed completely from manual labor. Now, suddenly, with the advent of automation, that dream has acquired a startling—and rather frightening—reality. Many scientists now say that within a few years all industry will be fully automated and that the new science of cybernetics will make human labor obsolete. Computers will run the world. What happens to men—and to society in general—when this occurs is something nobody knows. But it will almost certainly bring about social problems that should be brought to public attention immediately. So far, only a handful of experts are talking about the problems; the public is still largely unaware of the real meaning of automation.

With the second paragraph you take care of your *con* points and begin to use your references. Your cards are lined up and ready to go. Glance at the note on a card (or the notes on several cards related to the same point) and start building your own paragraph. Since this is the first draft, put your footnotes in the text as you go along, in abbreviated form, separated from your own words by triple parentheses. Don't number them yet. Remember, this is your first draft:

> To most people, automation is just a word that they associate vaguely with science fiction, or more vaguely still with faster production methods in large factories, or in a rather general way with such things as automatic washing machines, IBM cards, and zip codes. To others it represents "a mechanized, transistorized cornucopia which may someday free mankind from drudgery, fill his cupboard with abundance, and pave new highways to self-fulfillment." (((Newsweek, p. 73))) And certainly this potential exists. As Alice Mary Hilton points out, "a new era, the age of abundance and leisure, is being born." (((Hilton, p. 220))) But Miss Hilton goes on to ask the big question: "What happens to humanity when it is freed from the shackles of laboring in order to sustain life?" (((Hilton, p. 222))) And R. L. Heilbroner calls automation likely "the central controversy of American political and economic life for at least the next decade and maybe more." (((Heilbroner, p. 34)))

The triple parentheses make your abbreviated citations stand out from the text; you will replace these with footnote numbers when you write your final draft, and you will then also write out your citation in full and put it where it belongs—either at the bottom of the page or at the end of your manuscript, according to your instructor's preference. All you need to put between your triple parentheses at this point is the name of the author (or the name of the publication, if you are quoting from an unsigned article or editorial, as is the case above with *Newsweek* [1]) and the page numbers. When you are ready to type your final draft, it will be a simple matter to check your bibliography cards for all the details you need for the full citation—you will find, for example, that Hilton and Heilbroner have separate cards containing full information on the work cited.[2] Thus the triple parentheses provide you with an accurate key to your sources and simultaneously save a great deal of time—you needn't stop to worry at this point about taking care of worrisome mechanical details of punctuation.

Unless you do it this way you can bog down hopelessly in detail or get completely lost in numbers. The important thing,

---

[1] "The Challenge of Automation," *Newsweek*, Jan. 25, 1965, pp. 73–80.
[2] Alice Mary Hilton, "Cyberculture—the Age of Abundance and Leisure," *Michigan Quarterly Review*, III (Fall, 1964), pp. 217–229, and R. L. Heilbroner, "New Horizons in Economics," *Saturday Review*, Aug. 29, 1964, pp. 31–34.

in the first draft, is to keep your sources straight but to keep moving. So take advantage of the "triple parenthesis trick." It's quick, efficient, and accurate.

Define your terms. When you suggest, as in the sample paragraphs on automation, that the public does not adequately understand a terminology, or when you introduce new ideas that may be unfamiliar to your readers, your logical next step is to define your terms:

> Only by understanding exactly what the term "automation" means can the public understand the full extent of the problem . . .

Here your general background from the encyclopedias will be helpful. Since this is factual material and should be a matter of public knowledge (whether the public understands it or not), it will probably be unnecessary to quote sources if you write your explanation in your own words (only verbatim quotations and matters of opinion need to be documented). Your purpose in defining your terms is simply to make certain that your reader understands exactly what it is you intend to talk about.

Then you are ready to proceed with the main body of your argument. Move on through your cards, point by point, discussing, illustrating, explaining, pulling in your evidence:

> The basic problem, of course, is unemployment. If machines take over the jobs of men, it makes little difference how cheaply and efficiently machines can turn out products, for men will have no way to make the money to buy the products. Heilbroner points out that the new technology will displace not only factory workers but the people involved in the service and administrative end of production. (((Heilbroner, p. 31))) Edmund Berkeley describes an office in which computer-controlled machinery opens and reads the mail, answers it, sends orders to the factory where other machines make the product, package it, label it, and send it to the shipping room—all without human intervention. (((Berkeley, pp. 163–164))) Although the hope persists that automation will create as many new jobs as it destroys, most experts dismiss this as wishful thinking or simple ignorance. (((Newsweek, pp. 76–77, Hilton, p. 225)))

Follow the cards. Already divided into topics and subtopics, they will guide you, help you develop your own full paragraphs. Use specific examples, note differences in points of view among the authorities, weigh the evidence, make your judgment. Then tie the whole paper together with your conclusion (look back at your introduction for tips, as suggested on page 54), and you are ready for your final draft.

The Final Draft

First go through your rough draft, numbering each of the notes enclosed in triple parentheses. As you type your final copy, you will use this number, raising it slightly above the word it follows. Use only the number, not the parentheses or the note inside:

> Rough draft: Berkeley also points this out. (((Berkeley, p. 170)))
> Final draft: Berkeley also points this out.[7]

Raised numbers signal footnotes. A corresponding number appears with the footnote that tells the reader where you found your information—the exact publication and page number.

Traditionally, a footnote goes at the bottom of the page that carries its corresponding number; the footnote is single-spaced and separated from the text by a triple space. This can lead to such frustrating problems of spacing, however, that many instructors permit students to gather all their footnotes together on one page at the end of the term paper. The information in the footnotes is the same, regardless of position.

Rigid rules govern the preparation of footnotes, and they must be followed *exactly*. Your instructor will either supply you with a sheet of instructions or refer you to some standard guide for research papers. You should familiarize yourself in a general way with the conventions of preparing footnotes and bibliography, but it is pointless to attempt to memorize all the rules in detail. They are highly complicated, and the best way to make certain your footnotes are right is to make them match the standard models. Even very learned scholars who make a career of writing research papers usually work with a style sheet within easy reach. So should you.

Your bibliography—a list of all the works you have cited—goes on a page of its own at the end of your paper. Alphabetize your bibliography cards by authors' last names (or by the name of the work, if it is anonymous), and again follow instructions on your style sheet *exactly* in making out your list. No guesswork, no originality. Bibliographies, like footnotes, test your ability to follow detailed instructions, not your ability to write.

So do such housekeeping chores as numbering your pages and preparing your title page. These are matters handled differently by different instructors. Follow directions. That's part of your job.

Summary

Few students realize that the research methods they learn in writing the term paper have a far wider range than the classroom. Professional writers of nonfiction use substantially the same methods.

In the course of one year, one author may publish articles on any number of subjects—deep-sea diving, Czarist Russia, the garment industry, mountain climbing, stamp collecting, politics, fashions. He is most certainly not an authority on all these subjects, yet millions of readers accept his statements without doubting his right to speak with authority. Whatever his subject, he seems to have a thorough grasp of it, and indeed his information will be as reliable as it is interesting.

How does he do it? He researches. He goes to the library with his pen and his stack of note cards, he combs the encyclopedias and the indexes, and he reads and takes notes. In his final article he will not use footnotes, and his style may differ from yours in many ways, but he will gather his information exactly the way you gathered yours for your term paper. And he will be equally certain of its accuracy (the writer who is careless with his facts will very shortly find himself barred from any reputable magazine).

Furthermore, the businessman, the scientist, the lawyer, the careerist in any field who is asked to write something about his specialty for publication (as you may be asked, some day) will do exactly the same thing. Nobody carries in his head all the facts or all the interesting details of any subject (except, perhaps, himself—and even then he may miss a point or two). Anybody who writes for publication on any subject that depends upon a factual background or fully informed opinion must research his subject.

In short, he must use the library.

And that, if you have not already realized it, is perhaps the chief benefit you will receive from the preparation of a term paper. You have *used* the library. Many people never find out what that means. They may drop in on a library, they may wander through the stacks, they may even check out books—but they never really *use* the library. They don't really know what is there or how to find out. They are even a little afraid of libraries. And this in a country whose free public libraries are the wonder of the world.

If you have learned nothing else from writing a term paper, it will still have been a worthwhile experiment if it has taught you the value of a library and a few practical techniques of research. A trial thesis, a stack of cards, a pen—and the wilderness of books becomes a paradise of ordered paths when the techniques are mastered. Any question that occurs to you can be answered, insofar as man is able to provide answers, in the books and papers that libraries hold in their keeping.

You need only *to want to know*. That is the great thing. If you want to know, you can find out. Research is the key. The library is the great treasure house. Take advantage of it.

15
Summing Up

All writing—not just the writing we classify as literature, but all writing, from the most ordinary to the most sublime— springs from the very simple and very basic urge of human beings to communicate with each other. You write for the same reason you talk: because you have something to say. Oddly, that large and obvious truth is often overlooked or forgotten. Yet nothing else is as important as this to the writer who would improve his craft. The first principle of writing can be put into these four words: Have something to say.

That is where writing begins. And that is why so much of your early work in this book was with thesis and structure, with sifting and evaluating your ideas until you were certain of your own opinion on a subject, and then with developing that opinion into essay form. You learned, in short, to think before writing.

It was not easy work. Thinking is never easy. To many of you it must have seemed a slow, arduous, unglamorous, exasperating way of going about writing. But from that labor you should have emerged with something every writer must have if he is ever to express himself completely and clearly: a sense of structure.

And then you were ready to pursue that elusive thing called "style."

No book, of course, could supply you with all the elements that go into a writer's style, for ultimately your style reflects everything that you are—your attitudes, your capacity for thought and feeling, the whole quality of your mind and imagination. A book can only point out those elements of style that are common to all good writing and explain some of the techniques that experienced writers have learned to use, or use instinctively, in the practice of their craft. A book can supply guideposts, shortcuts, insights, advice, examples, exercises—all designed to help you say what you want to say with precision and grace.

That is what this book has tried to do.

In the process, it has required you to work very hard. You have had to break old habits and establish new ones. You have analyzed and invented and listened and read and written and rewritten. Moving from whole essay to paragraph to sentence to single words, and then back to whole essay again, building paragraphs, experimenting with every kind of sentence, searching for *le mot juste,* trying your hand at unfamiliar techniques, you have written many thousands of words. It has been a long and rigorous apprenticeship.

And of course it is not finished. A writer's apprenticeship to his craft is never finished. As long as you continue to write, you will continue to learn. But even after a year's apprenticeship you should be able to see a great improvement in your own work. No matter what your writing was like before you started—whether it was very good or very bad—it should be better now. You certainly have the right to expect that.

You can also expect some very tangible benefits as a student. You can expect to perform now at a higher level on any kind of writing assignment. Essay questions on examinations should never again look quite so forbidding. Term papers should have lost their terrors. If you are a college student, or if you are college bound, a great many term papers lie ahead of you. You are ready for them, not only with improved writing skills but with a knowledge of research methods.

And you can expect one other benefit—one that will last a lifetime, no matter how you spend your future: you will be a better reader. You will be able to see almost immediately what another writer is trying to do, what points he particularly wants to make, how he creates his effects. You will know these things because, as the saying goes, you have been there yourself. You will be able to spot bad writing in an instant—you are likely, in fact, to become a quite deadly critic. But you will also delight in good writing, because you know how it got that way. It all adds up to greater pleasure in reading.

But most important of all will be your own sure sense that you can communicate with others through written words, can say what you mean and say it well. It is a fine and exciting thing to learn how to handle with skill and assurance that most marvelous and complex and magical instrument, the English language. For language is the most splendid achievement of man, and it is a powerful instrument indeed. Use it with pride.

Handy Reminders

WHAT IS AN ESSAY?

An essay is the written expression of its author's opinion. Think before you write. Opinion always comes first.

FROM OPINION TO THESIS

The thesis of your essay is your opinion boiled down to one arguable statement.
The five-step process of finding a thesis is:
1. *Take inventory.*
2. *Ask questions.*
3. *Look for relationships.*
4. *Ask the yes-or-no question.*
5. *Qualify.*

THE FULL AND FINAL THESIS

Elements of a full thesis are:
1. *Thesis.*
2. *Points that can be made against your thesis.*
3. *Points in favor of your thesis.*

STRUCTURE

The function of the introductory paragraph is simply to introduce the subject and come to the point.

Whether your middle section is short or long, it is here that the real power of your essay resides. For the middle section is your argument.

To develop the middle section, you need only three rules to guide you:

1. Make the necessary concessions to the opposition as soon as possible.

2. Devote at least one full paragraph to every major pro argument in your full thesis statement.

3. Save your best argument for the last.

Your conclusion begins with the thesis and widens gradually toward a final broad statement.

FIRST STEPS TOWARD STYLE

For the time being:

1. Do not use first person.

2. Do not use the word "there"—ever.

THE SIZE AND SHAPE OF MIDDLE PARAGRAPHS

Like the essay itself, every paragraph has three parts: a beginning, a middle, and an end.

The pattern is the same one you use in speech: topic sentence, explanation and illustration, conclusion.

CONNECTIONS BETWEEN PARAGRAPHS

Transitions between paragraphs fall roughly into three categories:

1. Standard devices.

2. Paragraph hooks.

3. Combinations of #1 and #2.

THE PASSIVE VOICE

To avoid passive voice, make your subject do something.

THE SOUND OF SENTENCES

Written sentences should <u>sound</u> like natural speech, but they can't <u>be</u> natural speech.

The first principle of rhythm in writing, to capture the basic rhythm of speech, is variation in sentence length.

You must remember that a sentence is a thing of movable parts, an endlessly adaptable structure that is completely subject to the writer's will, shrinking or expanding to fit the sound and sense he chooses to give it.

PARALLEL STRUCTURE

A parallelism does not say the same thing in different words. The repetition is a repetition of <u>structure</u>.

Whenever a sentence contains two or more similar elements, these elements must be kept parallel, no matter how small.

If you repeat an article or a preposition once, repeat it every time—or not at all.

A WAY WITH WORDS

A metaphor never explains; it creates an image, and the image explains itself.

The principle for both metaphor and simile is the same: both of them make or imply a comparison between two things; one of the two things compared is literal, the other figurative.

MORE FREEDOM AND A FEW FLOURISHES

Irony is the art of using words that say one thing and mean another. Its purpose, however, is not to deceive but to make clear.

The paradox of writing in first person is that although you use the word "I" to tell your story, you are not really writing about yourself.

Index